Quick & Easy
Simple Chinese

p

Contents

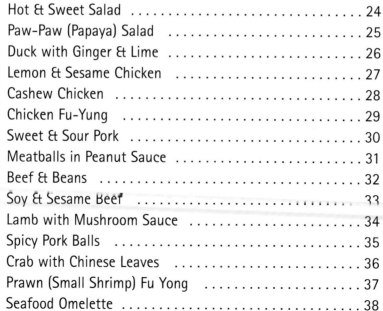

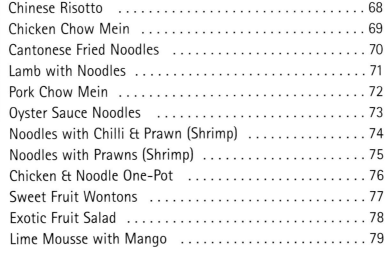

Introduction

The abundance of Chinese restaurants in the West demonstrates perfectly the popularity of Chinese cooking. Authentic dishes from all over China are assembled here for you to try at home. These recipes are delicious, incredibly easy to prepare and fortunately, for those with a busy lifestyle, many can be cooked in under an hour.

The Arrival of Chinese Cuisine

Chinese cuisine was introduced to the West when Chinese migrants settled in San Francisco during the Gold Rush. Since then, Chinese restaurants have spread throughout the world and Chinese ingredients and cooking equipment are now readily available.

Benefits of Eating Chinese

Chinese food is generally cooked rapidly over very high heat, using a minimum of oil, which preserves texture, flavour and nutrients. The ingredients include fish,

vegetables, and meats combined with noodles or rice, excellent sources of slow-energy releasing carbohydrates. High-cholesterol ingredients, such as dairy products and red meats, are used sparingly, if at all. Chinese meals are well-balanced, not only in terms of a healthy diet, but also in their aim to provide complementary courses: spicy dishes are served with sweet-and-sour alternatives, dry-cooked dishes are accompanied by those in sauces.

Regional Cuisine

China is a vast country with an enormous variety of different climates which affect the agricultural productivity within each area. The harsh climate around the capital of Beijing in the North is very different to the milder coastal areas of the South; the influence of the Yangtse river is felt strongly at its delta near Shanghai in the East, while the West enjoys a mild humid climate and rich fertile soil in the shadow of the Tien Shan mountains. The regional cuisines are equally diverse.

The North. Dishes from the North are strongly flavoured, using leeks, onions and garlic. Many dishes containing lamb, not pork, bear testimony to the Moslem culture introduced by invading Tartars from Central Asia. In northern areas wheat is used more frequently than rice, served as pancakes, noodles or dumplings.

The South. The first emigrant Chinese originated from Canton and its surrounding areas; this is still the most commonly known Chinese food in the West. Traditionally their foods, such as small fish, little parcels of meat or patties and dumplings are steam cooked. These include Dim Sum, which are served as snacks in teahouses.

The East. Benefiting enormously from the annual flooding of the Yangtze River, the East boasts very rich soil. The fertile plains allow growth of broccoli, sweet potatoes, pak choi, soya beans, tea, rice – the list is almost endless! Many of the traditional dishes are vegetarian and they vary enormously. Today, the regional cuisines of the east have been influenced by the city of Shanghai which has assimilated culinary influences from around the world. Dairy products have infiltrated Chinese kitchens, but duck, ham and fish in piquant spices still remain specialities.

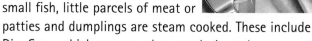
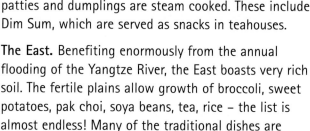

The West. Benefiting from a mild climate, Szechuan is noted for its robust, richly coloured spicy dishes. Szechuan cookery uses lots of garlic, ginger, onions, leeks and Szechuan peppercorns. Western China is renowned for its smoking, drying, pickling and salting techniques, used to preserve foods and enhance flavours.

Seven different ingredients are used to achieve seven very particular flavours in Szechuan cooking: sweet flavours use honey; salty ones, soy sauce; sour flavours, vinegar; bitter ones, onions or leeks; fragrant dishes, garlic or ginger; sesame flavours, sesame seed paste and hot recipes use chillies.

Ingredients

Chinese ingredients are widely available in supermarkets although it is worth investing in better quality versions of some of the oils, condiments and sauces from specialist shops.

Bamboo shoots. Bamboo shoots, although bland on their own, are used for their texture. To prepare fresh shoots, remove the tough outer skins and boil in water for 40–50 minutes.

Bean sauce. Available in cans or jars, this savoury paste is black or yellow and made from crushed, salted soya beans, flour and four spices. Red paste is used for sweet sauces.

Chillies. Fiery hot chilli oil contains chilli flakes and should be used with caution. Chilli bean sauce contains soya beans and uses the chillies for flavour – it should

also be used sparingly. If using fresh chillies remember that small pointed chillies are usually significantly hotter than larger, more rounded alternatives. The seeds are the hottest part so removing these will reduce the potency of the peppers.

Chinese five-spice. The five spices are: star anise, fennel seeds, cinnamon, cloves and Szechuan pepper. They produce a musty, pungent aroma and add a delicious and distinctive Chinese flavour to dishes when added sparingly.

Chinese rice wine and vinegar. Rice wine is made from glutinous rice and resembles dry sherry (which can be used as a suitable cooking alternative). Rice vinegar is distilled from Chinese rice wine and is stronger than red

vinegar. Cider or white wine vinegars can be used instead.

Dried mushrooms. Shiitake mushrooms have a strong flavour; they are expensive but a little goes a long way. The dried mushrooms need to be soaked for 20–30 minutes before use; the water can be kept for stock.

Ginger. Ginger root can be bought in the supermarket, look for plump pieces with shiny unblemished skin. Cut the amount you need, peel it then chop, slice or grate it. Fresh ginger will keep for weeks in a cool, dry place. Ground ginger is not a good substitute.

Hoisin sauce. Made from soya beans, sugar, flour, vinegar, chillies, garlic, sesame oil and salt. It is used for flavouring in small quantities combined with soy sauce or used alone on duck, spare ribs or seafood.

Lemon grass. The lower part of lemon grass stems add a slightly citrus flavour to a dish. It should be removed before serving if used whole.

Star anise. This is a star-shaped fruit with a strong aniseed flavour. Usually used ground, pods can be used although they should be removed before serving.

Cooking equipment

A good quality wok is essential if you want to achieve an authentic Chinese taste. Traditionally made from cast iron, there are now many different types: stainless steel woks are not recommended as they scorch, and some non-stick woks cannot tolerate the very high temperatures required. Food should be tossed or stirred continuously to cook evenly.

There are few special accessories required for Chinese cooking. A lid for your wok is essential for steaming. Clevers are used to chop, dice and cut everything from shellfish and herbs, to meat and vegetables. Chop sticks are used for preparation – they are unlikely to damage delicate food – as well as for eating.

KEY
Simplicity level 1 - 3 (1 easiest, 3 slightly harder)
Preparation time
Cooking time

Chinese Potato & Pork Broth

In this recipe the pork is seasoned with traditional Chinese flavourings – soy sauce, rice wine vinegar and a dash of sesame oil.

NUTRITIONAL INFORMATION

Calories	166	Sugars	.........2g
Protein	........10g	Fat	...........5g
Carbohydrate	...26g	Saturates	.......1g

5 MINS   20 MINS

SERVES 4

INGREDIENTS

1 litre/1¾ pints/4½ cups chicken stock

2 large potatoes, diced

2 tbsp rice wine vinegar

2 tbsp cornflour (cornstarch)

4 tbsp water

125 g/4½ oz pork fillet, sliced

1 tbsp light soy sauce

1 tsp sesame oil

1 carrot, cut into very thin strips

1 tsp ginger root, chopped

3 spring onions (scallions), sliced thinly

1 red (bell) pepper, sliced

225 g/8 oz can bamboo shoots, drained

VARIATION

For extra heat, add 1 chopped red chilli or 1 tsp of chilli powder to the soup in step 5.

1 Add the chicken stock, diced potatoes and 1 tbsp of the rice wine vinegar to a saucepan and bring to the boil. Reduce the heat until the stock is just simmering.

2 Mix the cornflour (cornstarch) with the water then stir into the hot stock.

3 Bring the stock back to the boil, stirring until thickened, then reduce the heat until it is just simmering again.

4 Place the pork slices in a dish and season with the remaining rice wine vinegar, the soy sauce and sesame oil.

5 Add the pork slices, carrot strips and ginger to the stock and cook for 10 minutes. Stir in the spring onions (scallions), red (bell) pepper and bamboo shoots. Cook for a further 5 minutes. Pour the soup into warmed bowls and serve immediately.

Chicken, Noodle & Corn Soup

The vermicelli gives this Chinese-style soup an Italian twist, but you can use egg noodles if you prefer.

NUTRITIONAL INFORMATION

Calories 401   Sugars 6g
Protein . . . . .31g   Fat 24g
Carbohydrate . . .17g   Saturates 13g

5 MINS   25 MINS

SERVES 4

INGREDIENTS

450 g/1 lb boned chicken breasts, cut into strips

1.2 litres/2 pints/5 cups chicken stock

150 ml/¼ pint/⅝ cup double (heavy) cream

100 g/3½ oz/¾ cup dried vermicelli

1 tbsp cornflour (cornstarch)

3 tbsp milk

175 g/6 oz sweetcorn (corn-on-the-cob) kernels

salt and pepper

finely chopped spring onion (scallions), to garnish (optional)

1 Put the chicken strips, chicken stock and double (heavy) cream into a large saucepan and bring to the boil over a low heat.

2 Reduce the heat slightly and simmer for about 20 minutes. Season the soup with salt and black pepper to taste.

3 Meanwhile, cook the vermicelli in lightly salted boiling water for 10-12 minutes, until just tender. Drain the pasta and keep warm.

4 In a small bowl, mix together the cornflour (cornstarch) and milk to make a smooth paste. Stir the cornflour

 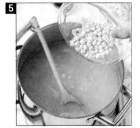 

(cornstarch) paste into the soup until thickened.

5 Add the sweetcorn (corn-on-the-cob) and vermicelli to the pan and heat through.

6 Transfer the soup to a warm tureen or individual soup bowls, garnish with spring onions (scallions), if desired, and serve immediately.

VARIATION

For crab and sweetcorn soup, substitute 450 g/1 lb cooked crabmeat for the chicken breasts. Flake the crabmeat well before adding it to the saucepan and reduce the cooking time by 10 minutes.

Mushroom Noodle Soup

A light, refreshing clear soup of mushrooms, cucumber and small pieces of rice noodles, flavoured with soy sauce and a touch of garlic.

NUTRITIONAL INFORMATION

Calories	84	Sugars 1g
Protein	.........1g	Fat 8g
Carbohydrate	....3g	Saturates 1g

 5 MINS   10 MINS

SERVES 4

INGREDIENTS

125 g/4½ oz flat or open-cup
   mushrooms

½ cucumber

2 spring onions (scallions)

1 garlic clove

2 tbsp vegetable oil

25 g/1 oz/¼ cup Chinese rice
   noodles

¾ tsp salt

1 tbsp soy sauce

1 Wash the mushrooms and pat dry on kitchen paper (paper towels). Slice thinly. Do not remove the peel as this adds more flavour.

2 Halve the cucumber lengthways. Scoop out the seeds, using a teaspoon, and slice the cucumber thinly.

3 Chop the spring onions (scallions) finely and cut the garlic clove into thin strips.

4 Heat the vegetable oil in a large saucepan or wok.

5 Add the spring onions (scallions) and garlic to the pan or wok and stir-fry for 30 seconds. Add the mushrooms and stir-fry for 2–3 minutes.

6 Stir in 600 ml/1 pint/2½ cups water. Break the noodles into short lengths and add to the soup. Bring to the boil, stirring occasionally.

7 Add the cucumber slices, salt and soy sauce, and simmer for 2–3 minutes.

8 Serve the mushroom noodle soup in warmed bowls, distributing the noodles and vegetables evenly.

COOK'S TIP

Scooping the seeds out from the cucumber gives it a prettier effect when sliced, and also helps to reduce any bitterness, but if you prefer, you can leave them in.

Prawn (Small Shrimp) Rolls

This variation of a spring roll is made with prawns (shrimps), stir-fried with shallots, carrot, cucumber, bamboo shoots and rice.

NUTRITIONAL INFORMATION

Calories	388	Sugars	........2g
Protein	.........9g	Fat	..........25g
Carbohydrate	...33g	Saturates	.......6g

10 MINS   15 MINS

SERVES 4

INGREDIENTS

2 tbsp vegetable oil

3 shallots, chopped very finely

1 carrot, cut into matchstick pieces

7 cm/3 inch piece of cucumber, cut into matchstick pieces

60 g/2 oz/½ cup bamboo shoots, shredded finely

125 g/4½ oz/½ cup peeled prawns (small shrimps)

90 g/3 oz/½ cup cooked long-grain rice

1 tbsp fish sauce or light soy sauce

1 tsp sugar

2 tsp cornflour (cornstarch), blended in 2 tbsp cold water

8 × 25 cm/10 inch spring roll wrappers

oil for deep-frying

salt and pepper

plum sauce, to serve

TO GARNISH

spring onion (scallion) brushes

sprigs of fresh coriander (cilantro)

1 Heat the oil in a wok and add the shallots, carrot, cucumber and bamboo shoots. Stir-fry briskly for 2–3 minutes. Add the prawns (shrimps) and cooked rice, and cook for a further 2 minutes. Season.

2 Mix together the fish sauce or soy sauce, sugar and blended cornflour (cornstarch). Add to the stir-fry and cook, stirring constantly, for about 1 minute, until thickened. Leave to cool slightly.

3 Place spoonfuls of the prawn (shrimp) and vegetable mixture on the spring roll wrappers. Dampen the edges and roll them up to enclose the filling completely.

4 Heat the oil for deep-frying and fry the spring rolls until crisp and golden brown. Drain on paper towels. Serve the rolls garnished with spring onion (scallion) brushes and fresh coriander (cilantro) and accompanied by the plum sauce.

Pork Dim Sum

These small steamed parcels are traditionally served as an appetizer and are very adaptable to your favourite fillings.

NUTRITIONAL INFORMATION

Calories 478	Sugars 3g
Protein 33g	Fat 29g
Carbohydrate . . .21g	Saturates 9g

 10 MINS   15 MINS

SERVES 4

INGREDIENTS

400 g/14 oz minced (ground) pork

2 spring onions (scallions), chopped

50 g/1¾ oz canned bamboo shoots, drained, rinsed and chopped

1 tbsp light soy sauce

1 tbsp dry sherry

2 tsp sesame oil

2 tsp caster (superfine) sugar

1 egg white, lightly beaten

4½ tsp cornflour (cornstarch)

24 wonton wrappers

1 Place the minced (ground) pork, spring onions (scallions), bamboo shoots, soy sauce, dry sherry, sesame oil, caster (superfine) sugar and beaten egg white in a large mixing bowl and mix until all the ingredients are thoroughly combined.

2 Stir in the cornflour (cornstarch), mixing until thoroughly incorporated with the other ingredients.

3 Spread out the wonton wrappers on a work surface (counter). Place a spoonful of the pork and vegetable mixture in the centre of each wonton wrapper and lightly brush the edges of the wrappers with water.

4 Bring the sides of the wrappers together in the centre of the filling, pinching firmly together.

5 Line a steamer with a clean, damp tea towel (dish cloth) and arrange the wontons inside.

6 Cover and steam for 5–7 minutes, until the dim sum are cooked through. Serve immediately.

COOK'S TIP

Bamboo steamers are designed to rest on the sloping sides of a wok above the water. They are available in a range of sizes.

Crispy Seaweed

This tasty Chinese starter is not all it seems – the 'seaweed' is in fact pak choi (bok choy) which is fried, salted and tossed with pine kernels.

NUTRITIONAL INFORMATION

Calories . . . . .214 Sugars 14g
Protein . . . . .6g Fat 15g
Carbohydrate . . .15g Saturates 2g

10 MINS   5 MINS

SERVES 4

INGREDIENTS

1 kg/2 lb 4 oz pak choi (bok choy)

groundnut oil, for deep-frying (about 850 ml/1½ pints/3¾ cups)

1 tsp salt

1 tbsp caster (superfine) sugar

50 g/1¾ oz/2½ tbsp toasted pine kernels (nuts)

1 Rinse the pak choi (bok choy) leaves under cold running water and then pat dry thoroughly with absorbent kitchen paper (paper towels).

2 Discarding any tough outer leaves, roll each pak choi leaf up, then slice

through thinly so that the leaves are finely shredded. Alternatively, use a food processor to shred the pak choi (bok choy).

3 Heat the groundnut oil in a large wok or heavy-based frying pan (skillet).

4 Carefully add the shredded pak choi (bok choy) leaves to the wok or frying pan (skillet) and fry for about 30 seconds or until they shrivel up and become crispy

(you will probably need to do this in several batches, depending on the size of the wok).

5 Remove the crispy seaweed from the wok with a slotted spoon and drain on absorbent kitchen paper (paper towels).

6 Transfer the crispy seaweed to a large bowl and toss with the salt, sugar and pine kernels (nuts). Serve immediately.

COOK'S TIP

The tough, outer leaves of pak choi (bok choy) are discarded as these will spoil the overall taste and texture of the dish.

Use savoy cabbage instead of the pak choi (bok choy) if it is unavailable, drying the leaves thoroughly before frying.

Chinese Omelette

This is a fairly filling omelette, as it contains chicken and prawns (shrimp). It is cooked as a whole omelette and then sliced for serving.

NUTRITIONAL INFORMATION

Calories 309   Sugars 0g
Protein . . . . .34g   Fat 19g
Carbohydrate . . .0.2g   Saturates 5g

5 MINS   5 MINS

SERVES 4

INGREDIENTS

8 eggs

225 g/8 oz/2 cups cooked chicken, shredded

12 tiger prawns (jumbo shrimp), peeled and deveined

2 tbsp chopped chives

2 tsp light soy sauce

dash of chilli sauce

2 tbsp vegetable oil

1 Lightly beat the eggs in a large mixing bowl.

2 Add the shredded chicken and tiger prawns (jumbo shrimp) to the eggs, mixing well.

3 Stir in the chopped chives, light soy sauce and chilli sauce, mixing well to combine all the ingredients.

4 Heat the vegetable oil in a large preheated frying pan (skillet) over a medium heat.

5 Add the egg mixture to the frying pan (skillet), tilting the pan to coat the base completely.

6 Cook over a medium heat, gently stirring the omelette with a fork, until the surface is just set and the underside is a golden brown colour.

7 When the omelette is set, slide it out of the pan, with the aid of a palette knife (spatula).

8 Cut the Chinese omelette into squares or slices and serve immediately. Alternatively, serve the omelette as a main course for two people.

VARIATION

You could add extra flavour to the omelette by stirring in 3 tablespoons of finely chopped fresh coriander (cilantro) or 1 teaspoon of sesame seeds with the chives in step 3.

Son-in-Law Eggs

This recipe is supposedly so called because it is an easy dish for a son-in-law to cook to impress his new mother-in-law!

NUTRITIONAL INFORMATION

Calories 229   Sugars 8g
Protein ....9g   Fat 18g
Carbohydrate ....8g   Saturates 3g

15 MINS   15 MINS

SERVES 4

I N G R E D I E N T S

6 eggs, hard-boiled (hard-cooked)
   and shelled

4 tbsp sunflower oil

1 onion, sliced thinly

2 fresh red chillies, sliced

2 tbsp sugar

1 tbsp water

2 tsp tamarind pulp

1 tbsp liquid seasoning, such
   as Maggi

rice, to serve

1 Prick the hard-boiled (hard-cooked) eggs 2 or 3 times with a cocktail stick (toothpick).

2 Heat the sunflower oil in a wok and fry the eggs until crispy and golden. Drain on absorbent kitchen paper (paper towels).

3 Halve the eggs lengthways and put on a serving dish.

4 Reserve one tablespoon of the oil, pour off the rest, then heat the tablespoonful in the wok. Cook the onion and chillies over a high heat until golden and slightly crisp. Drain on kitchen paper (paper towels).

5 Heat the sugar, water, tamarind pulp and liquid seasoning in the wok and simmer for 5 minutes until thickened.

6 Pour the sauce over the eggs and spoon over the onion and chillies. Serve immediately with rice.

COOK'S TIP

Tamarind pulp is sold in oriental stores, and is quite sour. If it is not available, use twice the amount of lemon juice in its place.

Aspagarus Parcels

These small parcels are ideal as part of a main meal and irresistible as a quick snack with extra plum sauce for dipping.

NUTRITIONAL INFORMATION

Calories 194	Sugars 2g
Protein 3g	Fat 16g
Carbohydrate 11g	Saturates 4g

 5 MINS   25 MINS

SERVES 4

I N G R E D I E N T S

100 g/3½ oz fine tip asparagus

1 red (bell) pepper, deseeded and thinly sliced

50 g/1¾ oz/½ cup bean sprouts

2 tbsp plum sauce

1 egg yolk

8 sheets filo pastry

oil, for deep-frying

1 Place the asparagus, (bell) pepper and beansprouts in a large mixing bowl.

2 Add the plum sauce to the vegetables and mix until well-combined.

3 Beat the egg yolk and set aside until required.

4 Lay the sheets of filo pastry out on to a clean work surface (counter).

5 Place a little of the asparagus and red (bell) pepper filling at the top end of each filo pastry sheet. Brush the edges of the filo pastry with a little of the beaten egg yolk.

6 Roll up the filo pastry, tucking in the ends and enclosing the filling like a spring roll. Repeat with the remaining filo sheets.

7 Heat the oil for deep-frying in a large preheated wok. Carefully cook the parcels, 2 at a time, in the hot oil for 4–5 minutes or until crispy.

8 Remove the parcels with a slotted spoon and leave to drain on absorbent kitchen paper (paper towels).

9 Transfer the parcels to warm serving plates and serve immediately.

COOK'S TIP

Be sure to use fine-tipped asparagus as it is more tender than the larger stems.

Oriental Salad

This colourful crisp salad has a fresh orange dressing and is topped with crunchy vermicelli.

NUTRITIONAL INFORMATION

Calories ....139 Sugars 8g
Protein ....5g Fat 7g
Carbohydrate ...15g Saturates 1g

10 MINS   5 MINS

SERVES 4

INGREDIENTS

25 g/1 oz/¼ cup dried vermicelli

½ head Chinese leaves (cabbage)

125 g/4½ oz/2 cups bean sprouts

6 radishes

125 g/4½ oz mangetout (snow peas)

1 large carrot

125 g/4½ oz sprouting beans

DRESSING

juice of 1 orange

1 tbsp sesame seeds, toasted

1 tsp honey

1 tsp sesame oil

1 tbsp hazelnut oil

1 Break the vermicelli into small strands. Heat a wok and dry-fry the vermicelli until lightly golden.

COOK'S TIP

Make your own sprouting beans by soaking mung and aduki beans overnight in cold water, drain and rinse. Place in a large jar covered with muslin to secure it. Lay the jar on its side and place in indirect light. For the next 3 days rinse the beans once each day in cold water until they are ready to eat.

2 Remove from the pan with a slotted spoon and set aside until required.

3 Using a sharp knife or food processor, shred the Chinese leaves (cabbage) and wash with the bean sprouts. Drain thoroughly and place the leaves and bean sprouts in a large mixing bowl.

4 Thinly slice the radishes. Trim the mangetout (snow peas) and cut each into 3 pieces. Cut the carrot into thin matchsticks. Add the sprouting beans and prepared vegetables to the bowl.

5 Place all the dressing ingredients in a screw-top jar and shake until well-blended. Pour over the salad and toss.

6 Transfer the salad to a serving bowl and sprinkle over the reserved vermicelli before serving.

Noodle & Mango Salad

Fruit combines well with the peanut dressing, (bell) peppers and chilli in this delicous hot salad.

NUTRITIONAL INFORMATION

Calories	368	Sugars	........11g
Protein	........11g	Fat	..........26g
Carbohydrate	...24g	Saturates	.......5g

15 MINS   5 MINS

SERVES 4

INGREDIENTS

250 g/9 oz thread egg noodles

2 tbsp groundnut oil

4 shallots, sliced

2 cloves garlic, crushed

1 red chilli, deseeded and sliced

1 red (bell) pepper, deseeded and sliced

1 green (bell) pepper, deseeded and sliced

1 ripe mango, sliced into thin strips

25 g/1 oz/¼ cup salted peanuts, chopped

DRESSING

4 tbsp peanut butter

100 ml/3½ fl oz/⅓ cup coconut milk

1 tbsp tomato purée (tomato paste)

1 Place the egg noodles in a large dish or bowl. Pour over enough boiling water to cover the noodles and leave to stand for 10 minutes.

2 Heat the groundnut oil in a large preheated wok or frying pan (skillet).

3 Add the shallots, crushed garlic, chilli and (bell) pepper slices to the wok or frying pan (skillet) and stir-fry for 2–3 minutes.

4 Drain the egg noodles thoroughly in a colander. Add the drained noodles and mango slices to the wok or frying pan

(skillet) and heat through for about 2 minutes.

5 Transfer the noodle and mango salad to warmed serving dishes and scatter with chopped peanuts.

6 To make the dressing, mix together the peanut butter, coconut milk and tomato purée (tomato paste) then spoon over the noodle salad. Serve immediately.

COOK'S TIP

If preferred, gently heat the peanut dressing before pouring over the noodle salad.

Prawn (Shrimp) Salad

Noodles and bean sprouts form the basis of this refreshing salad which combines the flavours of fruit and prawns (shrimp).

NUTRITIONAL INFORMATION

Calories	359	Sugars	........4g
Protein	........31g	Fat	..........15g
Carbohydrate	...25g	Saturates	.......2g

15 MINS   5 MINS

SERVES 4

INGREDIENTS

250 g/9 oz fine egg noodles

3 tbsp sunflower oil

1 tbsp sesame oil

1 tbsp sesame seeds

150 g/5½ oz/1½ cups bean sprouts

1 ripe mango, sliced

6 spring onions (scallions), sliced

75 g/2¾ oz radish, sliced

350 g/12 oz peeled cooked prawns (shrimp)

2 tbsp light soy sauce

1 tbsp sherry

1 Place the egg noodles in a large bowl and pour over enough boiling water to cover. Leave to stand for 10 minutes.

2 Drain the noodles thoroughly and pat dry with kitchen paper (paper towels).

COOK'S TIP

If fresh mango is unavailable, use canned mango slices, rinsed and drained, instead.

3 Heat the sunflower oil in a large wok or frying pan (skillet) and stir-fry the noodles for 5 minutes, tossing frequently.

4 Remove the wok from the heat and add the sesame oil, sesame seeds and bean sprouts, tossing to mix well.

5 In a separate bowl, mix together the sliced mango, spring onions (scallions), radish and prawns (shrimp). Stir in the light soy sauce and sherry and mix until thoroughly combined.

6 Toss the prawn (shrimp) mixture with the noodles and transfer to a serving dish. Alternatively, arrange the noodles around the edge of a serving plate and pile the prawn (shrimp) mixture into the centre. Serve immediately as this salad is best eaten warm.

Carrot & Coriander Salad

This tangy, crunchy salad makes an ideal accompaniment to many Chinese main courses.

NUTRITIONAL INFORMATION

Calories 50	Sugars 4g	
Protein 1g	Fat 3g	
Carbohydrate 5g	Saturates 0.4g	

 5 MINS   0 MINS

SERVES 4

INGREDIENTS

4 large carrots

2 celery sticks, cut into matchsticks

2 tbsp roughly chopped fresh coriander (cilantro)

DRESSING

1 tbsp sesame oil

1½ tbsp rice vinegar

½ tsp sugar

½ tsp salt

1 To create flower-shaped carrot slices, as shown, cut several grooves lengthways along each carrot before slicing it.

2 Slice each carrot into very thin slices, using the slicing cutter of a grater.

3 Combine the carrot, celery and coriander (cilantro) in a bowl.

4 To make the dressing, combine the sesame oil, rice vinegar, sugar and salt in a bowl.

5 Just before serving, toss the carrot, celery and coriander (cilantro) mixture in the dressing and transfer to a serving dish.

Hot & Sour Duck Salad

This is a lovely tangy salad, drizzled with a lime juice and fish sauce dressing. It makes a splendid starter or light main course dish.

NUTRITIONAL INFORMATION

Calories	236	Sugars	.........3g
Protein	........27g	Fat	..........10g
Carbohydrate	...10g	Saturates	.......3g

 40 MINS   5 MINS

SERVES 4

I N G R E D I E N T S

2 heads crisp salad lettuce, washed and separated into leaves

2 shallots, thinly sliced

4 spring onions (scallions), chopped

1 celery stick, finely sliced into julienne strips

5 cm/2 inch piece cucumber, cut into julienne strips

125 g/4½ oz bean sprouts

1 x 200 g/7 oz can water chestnuts, drained and sliced

4 duck breast fillets, roasted and sliced

orange slices, to serve

D R E S S I N G

3 tbsp fish sauce

1½ tbsp lime juice

2 garlic cloves, crushed

1 red chilli pepper, seeded and very finely chopped

1 green chilli pepper, seeded and very finely chopped

1 tsp palm or demerara (brown crystal) sugar

1 Place the lettuce leaves into a large mixing bowl. Add the sliced shallots, chopped spring onions (scallions), celery strips, cucumber strips, bean sprouts and sliced water chestnuts. Toss well to mix. Place the mixture on a large serving platter.

2 Arrange the duck breast slices on top of the salad in an attractive overlapping pattern.

3 To make the dressing, put the fish sauce, lime juice, garlic, chillies and sugar into a small saucepan. Heat gently, stirring constantly. Taste and adjust the piquancy if liked by adding more lime juice, or add more fish sauce to reduce the sharpness.

4 Drizzle the warm salad dressing over the duck salad and serve immediately with orange slices.

Chinese Chicken Salad

This is a refreshing dish suitable for a summer meal or light lunch.

NUTRITIONAL INFORMATION

Calories	162	Sugars	........3g
Protein	........15g	Fat	..........10g
Carbohydrate	....5g	Saturates	.......2g

25 MINS   10 MINS

SERVES 4

INGREDIENTS

225 g/8 oz skinless, boneless chicken breasts

2 tsp light soy sauce

1 tsp sesame oil

1 tsp sesame seeds

2 tbsp vegetable oil

125 g/4½ oz bean sprouts

1 red (bell) pepper, seeded and thinly sliced

1 carrot, cut into matchsticks

3 baby corn cobs, sliced

snipped chives and carrot matchsticks, to garnish

SAUCE

2 tsp rice wine vinegar

1 tbsp light soy sauce

dash of chilli oil

1 Place the chicken breasts in a shallow glass dish.

2 Mix together the soy sauce and sesame oil and pour over the chicken. Sprinkle with the sesame seeds and let stand for 20 minutes, turning the chicken over occasionally.

3 Remove the chicken from the marinade and cut the meat into thin slices.

4 Heat the vegetable oil in a preheated wok or large frying pan (skillet). Add the chicken and fry for 4–5 minutes, until cooked through and golden brown on both sides. Remove the chicken from the wok with a slotted spoon, set aside and leave to cool.

5 Add the bean sprouts, (bell) pepper, carrot and baby corn cobs to the wok and stir-fry for 2–3 minutes. Remove from the wok with a slotted spoon, set aside and leave to cool.

6 To make the sauce, mix together the rice wine vinegar, light soy sauce and chilli oil.

7 Arrange the chicken and vegetables together on a serving plate. Spoon the sauce over the salad, garnish with chives and carrot matchsticks and serve.

Hot Rice Salad

Nutty brown rice combines well with peanuts and a sweet and sour mixture of fruit and vegetables in this tangy combination.

NUTRITIONAL INFORMATION

Calories 464   Sugars 17g
Protein . . . . .15g   Fat 24g
Carbohydrate . . .52g   Saturates 4g

5 MINS   30 MINS

SERVES 4

I N G R E D I E N T S

300 g/10½ oz/1½ cups brown rice

1 bunch spring onions (scallions)

1 red (bell) pepper

125 g/4½ oz radishes

425 g/15 oz can pineapple pieces in natural juice, drained

125 g/4½ oz/2 cups bean sprouts

90 g/3 oz/¾ cup dry-roasted peanuts

D R E S S I N G

2 tbsp crunchy peanut butter

1 tbsp groundnut oil

2 tbsp light soy sauce

2 tbsp white wine vinegar

2 tsp clear honey

1 tsp chilli powder

½ tsp garlic salt

pepper

1 Put the rice in a pan and cover with water. Bring to the boil, then cover and simmer for 30 minutes until tender.

2 Meanwhile, chop the spring onions (scallions), using a sharp knife. Deseed and chop the red (bell) pepper and thinly slice the radishes.

3 To make the dressing, place the crunchy peanut butter, groundnut oil, light soy sauce, white wine vinegar, honey, chilli powder, garlic salt and pepper in a small bowl and whisk for a few seconds until well combined.

4 Drain the rice thoroughly and place in a heatproof bowl.

5 Heat the dressing in a small saucepan for 1 minute and then toss into the rice and mix well.

6 Working quickly, stir the pineapple pieces, spring onions (scallions), (bell) pepper, bean sprouts and peanuts into the mixture in the bowl.

7 Pile the hot rice salad into a warmed serving dish.

8 Arrange the radish slices around the outside of the salad and serve immediately.

Chicken & Paw-Paw Salad

Try this recipe with a selection of different fruits for an equally tasty salad.

NUTRITIONAL INFORMATION

Calories	408	Sugars 8g
Protein	........30g	Fat 28g
Carbohydrate	...10g	Saturates 5g

 5 MINS   15 MINS

SERVES 4

INGREDIENTS

4 skinless, boneless chicken breasts

1 red chilli, deseeded and chopped

30 ml/1 fl oz/1⅞ tbsp red wine vinegar

75 ml/3 fl oz/⅓ cup olive oil

1 paw-paw (papaya), peeled

1 avocado, peeled

125 g/4½ oz alfalfa sprouts

125 g/4½ oz bean sprouts

salt and pepper

TO GARNISH

diced red (bell) pepper

diced cucumber

1 Poach the chicken breasts in boiling water for about 15 minutes or until cooked through.

2 Remove the chicken with a slotted spoon and set aside to cool.

3 To make the dressing, combine the chilli, red wine vinegar and olive oil, season well with salt and pepper and set aside.

4 Place the chicken breasts on a chopping board. Using a very sharp knife, cut the chicken breasts across the grain into thin diagonal slices. Set aside.

5 Slice the paw-paw (papaya) and avocado to the same thickness as the chicken.

6 Arrange the slices of paw-paw (papaya) and avocado, together with the chicken, in an alternating pattern on four serving plates.

7 Arrange the alfalfa sprouts and bean sprouts on the serving plates and garnish with the diced red (bell) pepper and cucumber. Serve the salad with the dressing.

VARIATION

Try this recipe with peaches or nectarines instead of paw-paw (papaya).

Bean Sprout Salad

This is a very light dish and is ideal on its own for a summer meal or as a starter.

NUTRITIONAL INFORMATION

Calories 70   Sugars 5g
Protein . . . . .4g   Fat 3g
Carbohydrate . . . .7g   Saturates 0.5g

     10 MINS   5 MINS

SERVES 4

I N G R E D I E N T S

1 green (bell) pepper, seeded

1 carrot

1 celery stick

2 tomatoes, finely chopped

350 g/12 oz bean sprouts

1 small cucumber

1 garlic clove, crushed

dash of chilli sauce

2 tbsp light soy sauce

1 tsp wine vinegar

2 tsp sesame oil

16 fresh chives

1 Using a sharp knife, cut the green (bell) pepper, carrot and celery into matchsticks and finely chop the tomatoes.

2 Blanch the bean sprouts in boiling water for 1 minute. Drain well and rinse under cold water. Drain thoroughly again.

3 Cut the cucumber in half lengthways. Scoop out the seeds with a teaspoon and discard. Cut the flesh into matchsticks.

4 Mix the cucumber with the bean sprouts, green (bell) pepper, carrot, tomatoes and celery.

5 To make the dressing, mix together the garlic, chilli sauce, soy sauce, wine vinegar and sesame oil in a small bowl.

6 Pour the dressing over the vegetables, tossing well to coat.

7 Spoon the bean sprout salad into a serving dish or on to 4 individual serving plates. Garnish the salad with fresh chives and serve.

VARIATION

Substitute 350 g/12 oz cooked, cooled green beans or mangetout (snow peas) for the cucumber. Vary the bean sprouts for a different flavour. Try aduki (adzuki) bean or alfalfa sprouts, as well as the better-known mung and soya bean sprouts.

Hot & Sweet Salad

This salad is made by mixing fruit and vegetables with the sharp, sweet and fishy flavours of the dressing.

NUTRITIONAL INFORMATION

Calories 169	Sugars 8g
Protein 14g	Fat 8g
Carbohydrate 11g	Saturates 1g

🍲 15 MINS   🕐 0 MINS

SERVES 4

INGREDIENTS

250 g/9 oz white cabbage, finely shredded

2 tomatoes, skinned, seeded and chopped

250 g/9 oz cooked green beans, halved if large

125 g/4½ oz peeled prawns (shrimp)

1 paw-paw (papaya), peeled, seeded and chopped

1-2 fresh red chillies, seeded and very finely sliced

60 g/2 oz/scant ⅓ cup roasted salted peanuts, crushed

handful of lettuce or baby spinach leaves, shredded or torn into small pieces

DRESSING

4 tbsp lime juice

2 tbsp fish sauce

sugar, to taste

pepper

1 Mix the white cabbage with the tomatoes, green beans, prawns (shrimp), three-quarters of the paw-paw (papaya) and half of the chillies in a large mixing bowl.

2 Stir in two-thirds of the crushed peanuts and mix well.

3 Line the rim of a large serving plate with the lettuce or spinach leaves and pile the salad mixture into the centre of the leaves.

4 To make the dressing, beat the lime juice with the fish sauce and add sugar and pepper to taste. Drizzle over the salad.

5 Scatter the top with the remaining paw-paw (papaya), chillies and crushed peanuts. Serve at once.

COOK'S TIP

To skin tomatoes, make a cross at the base with a very sharp knife, then immerse in a bowl of boiling water for a few minutes. Remove with a slotted spoon and peel off the skin.

Paw-Paw (Papaya) Salad

Choose firm paw-paws – or papayas as they are sometimes called – for this delicious salad.

NUTRITIONAL INFORMATION

Calories 193	Sugars 11g
Protein 3g	Fat 15g
Carbohydrate ...12g	Saturates 2g

   10 MINS   0 MINS

SERVES 4

I N G R E D I E N T S

DRESSING

4 tbsp olive oil

1 tbsp fish sauce or light soy sauce

2 tbsp lime or lemon juice

1 tbsp dark muscovado sugar

1 tsp finely chopped fresh red or
   green chilli

SALAD

1 crisp lettuce

¼ small white cabbage

2 paw-paws (papayas)

2 tomatoes

25 g/1 oz/¼ cup roasted peanuts,
   chopped roughly

4 spring onions (scallions), trimmed
   and sliced thinly

basil leaves, to garnish

1 To make the dressing, whisk together the oil, fish sauce or soy sauce, lime or lemon juice, sugar and chilli. Set aside, stirring occasionally to dissolve the sugar.

2 Shred the lettuce and white cabbage, then toss together and arrange on a large serving plate.

3 Peel the paw-paws (papayas) and slice them in half. Scoop out the seeds, then slice the flesh thinly. Arrange on top of the lettuce and cabbage.

4 Soak the tomatoes in a bowl of boiling water for 1 minute, then lift out and peel. Remove the seeds and chop the flesh. Arrange on the salad leaves.

5 Scatter the peanuts and spring onions (scallions) over the top. Whisk the dressing and pour over the salad. Garnish with basil leaves and serve at once.

COOK'S TIP

Choose plain, unsalted peanuts and toast them under the grill (broiler) until golden to get the best flavour. Take care not to burn them, as they brown very quickly.

Duck with Ginger & Lime

Just the thing for a lazy summer day – roasted duck sliced and served with a dressing made of ginger, lime juice, sesame oil and fish sauce.

NUTRITIONAL INFORMATION

Calories	529	Sugars	.........3g
Protein	........38g	Fat	..........41g
Carbohydrate	....3g	Saturates	.......6g

20 MINS   25 MINS

SERVES 4

INGREDIENTS

3 boneless Barbary duck breasts, about 250 g/9 oz each

salt

DRESSING

125 ml/4 fl oz/½ cup olive oil

2 tsp sesame oil

2 tbsp lime juice

grated rind and juice of 1 orange

2 tsp fish sauce

1 tbsp grated ginger root

1 garlic clove, crushed

2 tsp light soy sauce

3 spring onions (scallions), finely chopped

1 tsp sugar

about 250 g/9 oz assorted salad leaves

orange slices, to garnish (optional)

1 Wash the duck breasts, dry on kitchen paper (paper towels), then cut in half. Prick the skin all over with a fork and season well with salt. Place the duck pieces, skin-side down, on a wire rack or trivet over a roasting tin (pan).

2 Cook the duck in a preheated oven for 10 minutes, then turn over and cook for a further 12-15 minutes, or until the duck is cooked, but still pink in the centre, and the skin is crisp.

3 To make the dressing, beat the olive oil and sesame oil with the lime juice, orange rind and juice, fish sauce, grated ginger root, garlic, light soy sauce, spring onions (scallions) and sugar until well blended.

4 Remove the duck from the oven, and allow to cool. Using a sharp knife, cut the duck into thick slices.

5 Add a little of the dressing to moisten and coat the duck.

6 To serve, arrange assorted salad leaves on a serving dish. Top with the sliced duck breasts and drizzle with the remaining salad dressing.

7 Garnish with orange slices, if using, then serve at once.

Lemon & Sesame Chicken

Sesame seeds have a strong flavour which adds nuttiness to recipes. They are perfect for coating these thin chicken strips.

NUTRITIONAL INFORMATION

Calories 273	Sugars 5g	
Protein 29g	Fat 13g	
Carbohydrate 11g	Saturates 3g	

10 MINS 10 MINS

SERVES 4

INGREDIENTS

4 boneless, skinless chicken breasts

1 egg white

25 g/1 oz/2 tbsp sesame seeds

2 tbsp vegetable oil

1 onion, sliced

1 tbsp demerara (brown crystal) sugar

finely grated zest and juice of 1 lemon

3 tbsp lemon curd

200 g/7 oz can water chestnuts, drained

lemon zest, to garnish

1 Place the chicken breasts between 2 sheets of cling film (plastic wrap) and pound with a rolling pin to flatten. Slice the chicken into thin strips.

2 Whisk the egg white until light and foamy. Dip the chicken strips into the egg white, then coat in the sesame seeds.

3 Heat the oil in a wok and stir-fry the onion for 2 minutes until softened.

4 Add the chicken to the wok and stir-fry for 5 minutes, or until the chicken turns golden.

5 Mix the sugar, lemon zest, lemon juice and lemon curd and add to the wok. Allow it to bubble slightly.

6 Slice the water chestnuts thinly, add to the wok and cook for 2 minutes. Garnish with lemon zest and serve hot.

COOK'S TIP

Water chestnuts are commonly added to Chinese recipes for their crunchy texture as they do not have a great deal of flavour.

Cashew Chicken

Yellow bean sauce is available from large supermarkets. Try to buy a chunky sauce rather than a smooth sauce for texture.

NUTRITIONAL INFORMATION

Calories	398	Sugars	.........2g
Protein	........31g	Fat	..........27g
Carbohydrate	....8g	Saturates	.......4g

10 MINS   15 MINS

SERVES 4

INGREDIENTS

450 g/1 lb boneless chicken breasts

2 tbsp vegetable oil

1 red onion, sliced

175 g/6 oz/1½ cups flat mushrooms, sliced

100 g/3½ oz/⅓ cup cashew nuts

75 g/2¾ oz jar yellow bean sauce

fresh coriander (cilantro), to garnish

egg fried rice or plain boiled rice, to serve

1 Using a sharp knife, remove the excess skin from the chicken breasts, if desired. Cut the chicken into small, bite-sized chunks.

2 Heat the vegetable oil in a preheated wok or frying pan (skillet).

3 Add the chicken to the wok and stir-fry for 5 minutes.

4 Add the red onion and mushrooms to the wok and continue to stir-fry for a further 5 minutes.

5 Place the cashew nuts on a baking tray (cookie sheet) and toast under a preheated medium grill (broiler) until just browning – toasting nuts brings out their flavour.

6 Toss the toasted cashew nuts into the wok together with the yellow bean sauce and heat through.

7 Allow the sauce to bubble for 2–3 minutes.

8 Transfer the chop suey to warm serving bowls and garnish with fresh coriander (cilantro). Serve hot with egg fried rice or plain boiled rice.

VARIATION

Chicken thighs could be used instead of the chicken breasts for a more economical dish.

Chicken Fu-Yung

Although commonly described as an omelette, a foo-yung ('white lotus petals') should use egg whites only to create a very delicate texture.

NUTRITIONAL INFORMATION

Calories 220   Sugars 1g
Protein . . . . .16g   Fat 14g
Carbohydrate . . . .7g   Saturates 3g

5 MINS   5 MINS

SERVES 4

I N G R E D I E N T S

175 g/6 oz chicken breast fillet, skinned

½ tsp salt

pepper

1 tsp rice wine or dry sherry

1 tbsp cornflour (cornstarch)

3 eggs

½ tsp finely chopped spring onions (scallions)

3 tbsp vegetable oil

125 g/4½ oz green peas

1 tsp light soy sauce

salt

few drops of sesame oil

1 Cut the chicken across the grain into very small, paper-thin slices, using a cleaver. Place the chicken slices in a shallow dish.

2 In a small bowl, mix together ½ teaspoon salt, pepper, rice wine or dry sherry and cornflour (cornstarch).

3 Pour the mixture over the chicken slices in the dish, turning the chicken until well coated.

4 Beat the eggs in a small bowl with a pinch of salt and the spring onions (scallions).

5 Heat the vegetable oil in a preheated wok, add the chicken slices and stir-fry for about 1 minute, making sure that the slices are kept separated.

6 Pour the beaten eggs over the chicken, and lightly scramble until set. Do not stir too vigorously, or the mixture will break up in the oil. Stir the oil from the bottom of the wok so that the foo-yung rises to the surface.

7 Add the peas, light soy sauce and salt to taste and blend well. Transfer to warm serving dishes, sprinkle with sesame oil and serve.

COOK'S TIP

If available, chicken goujons can be used for this dish: these are small, delicate strips of chicken which require no further cutting and are very tender.

Sweet & Sour Pork

This dish is a popular choice in Western diets, and must be one of the best known of Chinese recipes.

NUTRITIONAL INFORMATION

Calories	471	Sugars	.......47g
Protein	.......16g	Fat	.........13g
Carbohydrate	...77g	Saturates	.......2g

 10 MINS　　 20 MINS

SERVES 4

INGREDIENTS

150 ml/¼ pint/⅔ cup vegetable oil, for deep-frying

225 g/8 oz pork fillet (tenderloin), cut into 1-cm/½-inch cubes

1 onion, sliced

1 green (bell) pepper, seeded and sliced

225 g/8 oz pineapple pieces

1 small carrot, cut into thin strips

25 g/1 oz canned bamboo shoots, drained, rinsed and halved

rice or noodles, to serve

BATTER

125 g/4½ oz/1 cup plain (all-purpose) flour

1 tbsp cornflour (cornstarch)

1½ tsp baking powder

1 tbsp vegetable oil

SAUCE

125 g/4½ oz/⅔ cup light brown sugar

2 tbsp cornflour (cornstarch)

125 ml/4 fl oz/½ cup white wine vinegar

2 garlic cloves, crushed

4 tbsp tomato purée (paste)

6 tbsp pineapple juice

1 To make the batter, sift the plain (all-purpose) flour into a mixing bowl, together with the cornflour (cornstarch) and baking powder. Add the vegetable oil and stir in enough water to make a thick, smooth batter (about 175 ml/6 fl oz/ ¾ cup).

2 Pour the vegetable oil into a preheated wok and heat until almost smoking.

3 Dip the cubes of pork into the batter, and cook in the hot oil, in batches, until the pork is cooked through. Remove the pork from the wok with a slotted spoon and drain on absorbent kitchen paper (paper towels). Set aside and keep warm until required.

4 Drain all but 1 tablespoon of oil from the wok and return it to the heat. Add the onion, (bell) pepper, pineapple pieces, carrot and bamboo shoots and stir-fry for 1–2 minutes. Remove from the wok with a slotted spoon and set aside.

5 Mix all of the sauce ingredients together and pour into the wok. Bring to the boil, stirring until thickened and clear. Cook for 1 minute, then return the pork and vegetables to the wok. Cook for a further 1–2 minutes, then transfer to a serving plate and serve with rice or noodles.

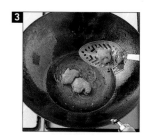

Meatballs in Peanut Sauce

Choose very lean minced (ground) beef to make these meatballs – or better still, buy some lean beef and mince (grind) it yourself.

NUTRITIONAL INFORMATION

Calories	553	Sugars	........10g
Protein	........32g	Fat	.........43g
Carbohydrate	...21g	Saturates	......12g

5 MINS   30 MINS

SERVES 4

I N G R E D I E N T S

500 g/1 lb 2 oz/2 cups lean minced (ground) beef

2 tsp finely grated fresh ginger root

1 small red chilli, deseeded and chopped finely

1 tbsp chopped fresh basil or coriander (cilantro)

1 tbsp sesame oil

1 tbsp vegetable oil

salt and pepper

S A U C E

2 tbsp red curry paste

300 ml/½ pint/1¼ cups coconut milk

125 g/4½ oz/1 cup ground peanuts

1 tbsp fish sauce

T O   G A R N I S H

chopped fresh basil

sprigs of fresh basil or coriander (cilantro)

VARIATION

Minced (ground) lamb makes a delicious alternative to beef. If you do use lamb, try substituting ground almonds for the peanuts and fresh mint for the basil.

1 Put the beef, ginger, chilli and basil or coriander (cilantro) into a food processor or blender. Add $^{1}/_{2}$ teaspoon of salt and plenty of pepper. Process for about 10–15 seconds until finely chopped. Alternatively, chop the ingredients finely and mix together.

2 Form the beef mixture into about 12 balls. Heat the sesame oil and vegetable oil in a wok or frying pan (skillet) and fry the meatballs over a medium-high heat until well browned on all sides, about 10 minutes. Lift them out and drain on kitchen paper (paper towels).

3 To make the sauce, stir-fry the red curry paste in the wok or frying pan (skillet) for 1 minute. Add the coconut milk, peanuts and fish sauce. Heat, stirring, until just simmering.

4 Return the meatballs to the wok or frying pan (skillet) and cook gently in the sauce for 10–15 minutes. If the sauce begins to get too thick, add a little extra coconut milk or water. Season with a little salt and pepper, according to taste.

5 Serve garnished with chopped fresh basil and sprigs of fresh basil or coriander (cilantro).

Beef & Beans

The green of the beans complements the dark colour of the beef, served in a rich sauce.

NUTRITIONAL INFORMATION

Calories	381	Sugars	.........3g
Protein	........25g	Fat	..........27g
Carbohydrate	...10g	Saturates	.......8g

 35 MINS   15 MINS

SERVES 4

INGREDIENTS

450 g/1 lb rump or fillet steak, cut into 2.5-cm/1-inch pieces

MARINADE

2 tsp cornflour (cornstarch)

2 tbsp dark soy sauce

2 tsp peanut oil

SAUCE

2 tbsp vegetable oil

3 garlic cloves, crushed

1 small onion, cut into 8

225 g/8 oz thin green beans, halved

25 g/1 oz/¼ cup unsalted cashews

25 g/1 oz canned bamboo shoots, drained and rinsed

2 tsp dark soy sauce

2 tsp Chinese rice wine or dry sherry

125 ml/4 fl oz/½ cup beef stock

2 tsp cornflour (cornstarch)

4 tsp water

salt and pepper

1 To make the marinade, mix together the cornflour (cornstarch), soy sauce and peanut oil.

2 Place the steak in a shallow glass bowl. Pour the marinade over the steak, turn to coat thoroughly, cover and leave to marinate in the refrigerator for at least 30 minutes.

3 To make the sauce, heat the oil in a preheated wok. Add the garlic, onion, beans, cashews and bamboo shoots and stir-fry for 2–3 minutes.

4 Remove the steak from the marinade, drain, add to the wok and stir-fry for 3–4 minutes.

5 Mix the soy sauce, Chinese rice wine or sherry and beef stock together. Blend the cornflour (cornstarch) with the water and add to the soy sauce mixture, mixing to combine.

6 Stir the mixture into the wok and bring the sauce to the boil, stirring until thickened and clear. Reduce the heat and leave to simmer for 2–3 minutes. Season to taste and serve immediately.

Soy & Sesame Beef

Soy sauce and sesame seeds are classic ingredients in Chinese cookery. Use a dark soy sauce for fuller flavour and richness.

NUTRITIONAL INFORMATION

Calories 324   Sugars 2g
Protein . . . . .25g   Fat 22g
Carbohydrate . . . .3g   Saturates 6g

5 MINS   10 MINS

SERVES 4

I N G R E D I E N T S

25 g/1 oz/2 tbsp sesame seeds

450 g/1 lb beef fillet

2 tbsp vegetable oil

1 green (bell) pepper, deseeded and thinly sliced

4 cloves garlic, crushed

2 tbsp dry sherry

4 tbsp soy sauce

6 spring onions (scallions), sliced

noodles, to serve

1 Heat a large wok or heavy-based frying pan (skillet) until it is very hot.

2 Add the sesame seeds to the wok or frying pan (skillet) and dry fry, stirring, for 1–2 minutes or until they just begin to brown. Remove the sesame seeds from the wok and set aside until required.

3 Using a sharp knife or meat cleaver, thinly slice the beef.

4 Heat the vegetable oil in the wok or frying pan (skillet). Add the beef and stir-fry for 2–3 minutes or until sealed on all sides.

5 Add the sliced (bell) pepper and crushed garlic to the wok and continue stir-frying for 2 minutes.

6 Add the dry sherry and soy sauce to the wok together with the spring onions (scallions). Allow the mixture in the wok to bubble, stirring occasionally, for about 1 minute, but do not let the mixture burn.

7 Transfer the garlic beef stir-fry to warm serving bowls and scatter with the dry-fried sesame seeds. Serve hot with boiled noodles.

COOK'S TIP

You can spread the sesame seeds out on a baking tray (cookie sheet) and toast them under a preheated grill (broiler) until browned all over, if you prefer.

Lamb with Mushroom Sauce

Use a lean cut of lamb, such as fillet, for this recipe for both flavour and tenderness.

NUTRITIONAL INFORMATION

Calories 219   Sugars 1g
Protein . . . . .21g   Fat 14g
Carbohydrate . . . .4g   Saturates 4g

5 MINS   10 MINS

SERVES 4

I N G R E D I E N T S

350 g/12 oz lean boneless lamb, such as
  fillet or loin

2 tbsp vegetable oil

3 garlic cloves, crushed

1 leek, sliced

175 g/6 oz large mushrooms, sliced

½ tsp sesame oil

fresh red chillies, to garnish

S A U C E

1 tsp cornflour (cornstarch)

4 tbsp light soy sauce

3 tbsp Chinese rice wine or dry sherry

3 tbsp water

½ tsp chilli sauce

1 Using a sharp knife or meat cleaver, cut the lamb into thin strips.

2 Heat the vegetable oil in a preheated wok or large frying pan (skillet).

3 Add the lamb strips, garlic and leek and stir-fry for about 2–3 minutes.

4 To make the sauce, mix together the cornflour (cornstarch), soy sauce, Chinese rice wine or dry sherry, water and chilli sauce and set aside.

5 Add the sliced mushrooms to the wok and stir-fry for 1 minute.

6 Stir in the prepared sauce and cook for 2–3 minutes, or until the lamb is cooked through and tender.

7 Sprinkle the sesame oil over the top and transfer the lamb and mushrooms to a warm serving dish. Garnish with red chillies and serve immediately.

VARIATION

The lamb can be replaced with lean steak or pork fillet (tenderloin) in this classic recipe from Beijing. You could also use 2–3 spring onions (scallions), 1 shallot or 1 small onion instead of the leek, if you prefer.

Spicy Pork Balls

These small meatballs are packed with flavour and cooked in a crunchy tomato sauce for a very quick dish.

NUTRITIONAL INFORMATION

Calories 299	Sugars 3g
Protein 28g	Fat 15g
Carbohydrate . . .14g	Saturates 4g

🍳 10 MINS   🕐 40 MINS

SERVES 4

I N G R E D I E N T S

450 g/1 lb minced (ground) pork

2 shallots, finely chopped

2 cloves garlic, crushed

1 tsp cumin seeds

½ tsp chilli powder

25 g/1 oz/½ cup wholemeal breadcrumbs

1 egg, beaten

2 tbsp sunflower oil

400 g/14 oz can chopped tomatoes, flavoured with chilli

2 tbsp soy sauce

200 g/7 oz can water chestnuts, drained

3 tbsp chopped fresh coriander (cilantro)

COOK'S TIP

Add a few teaspoons of chilli sauce to a tin of chopped tomatoes, if you can't find the flavoured variety.

1 Place the minced (ground) pork in a large mixing bowl. Add the shallots, garlic, cumin seeds, chilli powder, breadcrumbs and beaten egg and mix together well.

2 Form the mixture into balls between the palms of your hands.

3 Heat the oil in a large preheated wok. Add the pork balls and stir-fry, in batches, over a high heat for about 5 minutes or until sealed on all sides.

4 Add the tomatoes, soy sauce and water chestnuts and bring to the boil. Return the pork balls to the wok, reduce the heat and leave to simmer for 15 minutes.

5 Scatter with chopped fresh coriander (cilantro) and serve hot.

Crab with Chinese Leaves

The delicate flavour of Chinese leaves (cabbage) and crab meat are enhanced by the coconut milk in this recipe.

NUTRITIONAL INFORMATION

Calories	109	Sugars	.........1g
Protein	........11g	Fat	..........6g
Carbohydrate	....2g	Saturates	.......1g

5 MINS   10 MINS

SERVES 4

I N G R E D I E N T S

225 g/8 oz shiitake mushrooms

2 tbsp vegetable oil

2 cloves garlic, crushed

6 spring onions (scallions), sliced

1 head Chinese leaves (cabbage), shredded

1 tbsp mild curry paste

6 tbsp coconut milk

200 g/7 oz can white crab meat, drained

1 tsp chilli flakes

1 Using a sharp knife, cut the mushrooms into slices.

2 Heat the vegetable oil in a large preheated wok or heavy-based frying pan (skillet).

3 Add the mushrooms and garlic to the wok or frying pan (skillet) and stir-fry for 3 minutes or until the mushrooms have softened.

4 Add the spring onions (scallions) and shredded Chinese leaves (cabbage) to the wok and stir-fry until the leaves have wilted.

5 Mix together the mild curry paste and coconut milk in a small bowl.

6 Add the curry paste and coconut milk mixture to the wok, together with the crab meat and chilli flakes. Mix together until well combined.

7 Heat the mixture in the wok until the juices start to bubble.

8 Transfer the crab and vegetable stir-fry to warm serving bowls and serve immediately.

COOK'S TIP

Shiitake mushrooms are now readily available in the fresh vegetable section of most large supermarkets.

Prawn (Shrimp) Fu Yong

The classic ingredients of this popular dish are eggs, carrots and prawns (shrimps). Add extra ingredients such as peas or crabmeat, if desired.

NUTRITIONAL INFORMATION

Calories 240	Sugars 1g
Protein 22g	Fat 16g
Carbohydrate 1g	Saturates 3g

5 MINS   10 MINS

SERVES 4

I N G R E D I E N T S

2 tbsp vegetable oil

1 carrot, grated

5 eggs, beaten

225 g/8 oz raw prawn (small shrimp), peeled

1 tbsp light soy sauce

pinch of Chinese five-spice powder

2 spring onions (scallions), chopped

2 tsp sesame seeds

1 tsp sesame oil

COOK'S TIP

If only cooked prawns (shrimp) are available, add them just before the end of cooking, but make sure they are fully incorporated into the fu yong. They require only heating through. Overcooking will make them chewy and tasteless.

1 Heat the vegetable oil in a preheated wok or frying pan (skillet), swirling it around until the oil is really hot.

2 Add the grated carrot and stir-fry for 1–2 minutes.

3 Push the carrot to one side of the wok or frying pan (skillet) and add the beaten eggs. Cook, stirring gently, for 1–2 minutes.

4 Stir the prawns (small shrimp), light soy sauce and five-spice powder into the mixture in the wok. Stir-fry the mixture for 2–3 minutes, or until the (small) shrimps change colour and the mixture is almost dry.

5 Turn the prawn (small shrimp) fu yong out on to a warm plate and sprinkle the spring onions (scallions), sesame seeds and sesame oil on top. Serve immediately.

Seafood Omelette

This delicious omelette is filled with a mixture of fresh vegetables, sliced squid and prawns (shrimp).

NUTRITIONAL INFORMATION

Calories	216	Sugars	. . . . .2g
Protein	. . . . .20g	Fat	. . . . .13g
Carbohydrate	. . . .4g	Saturates	. . . . . . .4g

5 MINS   10 MINS

SERVES 4

I N G R E D I E N T S

4 eggs

3 tbsp milk

1 tbsp fish sauce or light soy sauce

1 tbsp sesame oil

3 shallots, sliced finely

1 small red (bell) pepper, cored, deseeded and sliced very finely

1 small leek, trimmed and cut into matchstick pieces

125 g/4½ oz squid rings

125 g/4½ oz/⅔ cup cooked peeled prawns (shrimp)

1 tbsp chopped fresh basil

15 g/½oz/1 tbsp butter

salt and pepper

sprigs of fresh basil, to garnish

1 Beat the eggs, milk and fish sauce or soy sauce together.

2 Heat the sesame oil in a wok or large frying pan (skillet) and add the shallots, (bell) pepper and leek. Stir-fry briskly for 2–3 minutes.

3 Add the squid rings, prawns (shrimp) and chopped basil to the wok or frying pan (skillet). Stir-fry for a further 2–3 minutes, until the squid looks opaque.

4 Season the mixture in the wok with salt and pepper to taste. Transfer to a warmed plate and keep warm until required.

5 Melt the butter in a large omelette pan or frying pan (skillet) and add the beaten egg mixture. Cook over a medium-high heat until just set.

6 Spoon the vegetable and seafood mixture in a line down the middle of the omelette, then fold each side of the omelette over.

7 Transfer the omelette to a warmed serving dish and cut into 4 portions. Garnish with sprigs of fresh basil and serve at once.

VARIATION

Chopped, cooked chicken makes a delicious alternative to the squid.

Use fresh coriander (cilantro) instead of the basil, if desired.

Trout with Pineapple

Pineapple is widely used in Chinese cooking. The tartness of fresh pineapple complements fish particularly well.

NUTRITIONAL INFORMATION

Calories 243	Sugars 4g
Protein 30g	Fat 11g
Carbohydrate 6g	Saturates 2g

5 MINS   15 MINS

SERVES 4

I N G R E D I E N T S

4 trout fillets, skinned

2 tbsp vegetable oil

2 garlic cloves, cut into slivers

4 slices fresh pineapple, peeled and diced

1 celery stick, sliced

1 tbsp light soy sauce

50 ml/2 fl oz/¼ cup fresh or unsweetened pineapple juice

150 ml/¼ pint/⅔ cup fish stock

1 tsp cornflour (cornstarch)

2 tsp water

shredded celery leaves and fresh red chilli slices, to garnish

1 Cut the trout fillets into strips. Heat 1 tablespoon of the vegetable oil in a preheated wok until almost smoking. Reduce the heat slightly, add the fish and sauté for 2 minutes. Remove from the wok and set aside.

2 Add the remaining oil to the wok, reduce the heat and add the garlic, diced pineapple and celery. Stir-fry for 1–2 minutes.

3 Add the soy sauce, pineapple juice and fish stock to the wok. Bring to the boil and cook, stirring, for 2–3 minutes, or until the sauce has reduced.

4 Blend the cornflour (cornstarch) with the water to form a paste and stir it into the wok. Bring the sauce to the boil and cook, stirring constantly, until the sauce thickens and clears.

5 Return the fish to the wok, and cook, stirring gently, until heated through. Transfer to a warmed serving dish and serve, garnished with shredded celery leaves and red chilli slices.

VARIATION

Use canned pineapple instead of fresh pineapple if you wish, choosing slices in unsweetened, natural juice in preference to a syrup.

Fish with Ginger Butter

Whole mackerel or trout are stuffed with herbs, wrapped in foil, baked and then drizzled with a fresh ginger butter.

NUTRITIONAL INFORMATION

Calories 328	Sugar 0g	
Protein 24g	Fat 25g	
Carbohydrate 1g	Saturates 13g	

10 MINS   30 MINS

SERVES 4

INGREDIENTS

4 x 250 g/9 oz whole trout or mackerel, gutted

4 tbsp chopped fresh coriander (cilantro)

5 garlic cloves, crushed

2 tsp grated lemon or lime zest

2 tsp vegetable oil

banana leaves, for wrapping (optional)

90 g/3 oz/6 tbsp butter

1 tbsp grated ginger root

1 tbsp light soy sauce

salt and pepper

coriander (cilantro) sprigs and lemon or lime wedges, to garnish

1 Wash and dry the fish. Mix the coriander (cilantro) with the garlic, lemon or lime zest and salt and pepper to taste. Spoon into the fish cavities.

2 Brush the fish with a little oil, season well and place each fish on a double thickness sheet of baking parchment or foil and wrap up well to enclose. Alternatively, wrap in banana leaves.

3 Place on a baking tray (cookie sheet) and bake in a preheated oven for about 25 minutes or until the flesh will flake easily.

4 Meanwhile, melt the butter in a small pan. Add the ginger and mix well.

5 Stir the light soy sauce into the saucepan.

6 To serve, unwrap the fish parcels, drizzle over the ginger butter and garnish with coriander (cilantro) and lemon or lime wedges.

COOK'S TIP

For a really authentic touch, wrap the fish in banana leaves, which can be ordered from specialist oriental supermarkets. They are not edible, but impart a delicate flavour to the fish.

Seafood Medley

Use any combination of fish and seafood in this delicious dish of coated fish served in a wine sauce.

NUTRITIONAL INFORMATION

Calories	168	Sugars	........2g
Protein	........29g	Fat	..........3g
Carbohydrate	....4g	Saturates	.......1g

5 MINS   15 MINS

SERVES 4

I N G R E D I E N T S

2 tbsp dry white wine

1 egg white, lightly beaten

½ tsp Chinese five-spice powder

1 tsp cornflour (cornstarch)

300 g/10½ oz raw prawns (shrimp),
   peeled and deveined

125 g/4½ oz prepared squid,
   cut into rings

125 g/4½ oz white fish fillets,
   cut into strips

vegetable oil, for deep-frying

1 green (bell) pepper, seeded and
   cut into thin strips

1 carrot, cut into thin strips

4 baby corn cobs, halved lengthways

1 Mix the wine, egg white, five-spice powder and cornflour (cornstarch) in a large bowl. Add the prawns (shrimp), squid rings and fish fillets and stir to coat evenly. Remove the fish and seafood with a slotted spoon, reserving any leftover cornflour (cornstarch) mixture.

2 Heat the oil in a preheated wok and deep-fry the prawns (shrimp), squid and fish for 2–3 minutes. Remove the seafood mixture from the wok with a slotted spoon and set aside.

3 Pour off all but 1 tablespoon of oil from the wok and return to the heat. Add the (bell) pepper, carrot and corn cobs and stir-fry for 4–5 minutes.

4 Return the seafood to the wok with any remaining cornflour (cornstarch) mixture. Heat through, stirring, and serve.

COOK'S TIP

Open up the squid rings and using a sharp knife, score a lattice pattern on the flesh to make them look attractive.

Prawns with Vegetables

This colourful and delicious dish is cooked with vegetables: vary them according to seasonal availability.

NUTRITIONAL INFORMATION

Calories ....298 Sugars 1g
Protein ....13g Fat 26g
Carbohydrate ....3g Saturates 3g

5 MINS   10 MINS

SERVES 4

INGREDIENTS

60 g/2 oz mangetout (snow peas)

½ small carrot

60 g/2 oz baby sweetcorn

60 g/2 oz straw mushrooms

175-250 g/6-9 oz raw tiger prawns
(jumbo shrimp), peeled

1 tsp salt

½ egg white, lightly beaten

1 tsp cornflour (cornstarch) paste

about 300 ml/½ pint/1¼ cups
vegetable oil

1 spring onion (scallion), cut into
short sections

4 slices ginger root, peeled and finely
chopped

½ tsp sugar

1 tbsp light soy sauce

1 tsp Chinese rice wine or dry sherry

a few drops sesame oil

lemon slices and chopped fresh chives,
to garnish

1 Using a sharp knife, top and tail the mangetout (snow peas); cut the carrot into the same size as the mangetout (snow peas); halve the baby sweetcorn and straw mushrooms.

2 Mix the prawns (shrimp) with a pinch of the salt, the egg white and cornflour (cornstarch) paste until the prawns (shrimp) are evenly coated.

3 Preheat a wok over a high heat for 2-3 minutes, then add the vegetable oil and heat to medium-hot.

4 Add the prawns (shrimp) to the wok, stirring to separate them. Remove the prawns (shrimp) with a slotted spoon as soon as the colour changes.

5 Pour off the oil, leaving about 1 tablespoon in the wok. Add the mangetout (snow peas), carrot, sweetcorn, mushrooms and spring onions (scallions).

6 Add the prawns (shrimp) together with the ginger, sugar, soy sauce and wine or sherry, blending well.

7 Sprinkle with the sesame oil and serve hot, garnished with lemon slices and chopped fresh chives.

Fish with Black Bean Sauce

Steaming is one of the preferred methods of cooking whole fish in China as it maintains both the flavour and the texture.

NUTRITIONAL INFORMATION

Calories ....292 Sugars 3g
Protein ....44g Fat 7g
Carbohydrate ....6g Saturates 0.4g

  10 MINS   🕙 10 MINS

SERVES 4

I N G R E D I E N T S

900 g/2 lb whole snapper, cleaned and scaled

3 garlic cloves, crushed

2 tbsp black bean sauce

1 tsp cornflour (cornstarch)

2 tsp sesame oil

2 tbsp light soy sauce

2 tsp caster (superfine) sugar

2 tbsp dry sherry

1 small leek, shredded

1 small red (bell) pepper, seeded and cut into thin strips

shredded leek and lemon wedges, to garnish

boiled rice or noodles, to serve

1 Rinse the fish inside and out with cold running water and pat dry with kitchen paper (paper towels).

2 Make 2-3 diagonal slashes in the flesh on each side of the fish, using a sharp knife. Rub the garlic into the fish.

3 Mix together the black bean sauce, cornflour (cornstarch), sesame oil, light soy sauce, sugar and dry sherry.

4 Place the fish in a shallow heatproof dish and pour the sauce mixture over the top. Sprinkle the shredded leek and (bell) pepper strips on top of the sauce.

5 Place the dish in the top of a steamer, cover and steam for 10 minutes, or until the fish is cooked through.

6 Transfer the fish to a serving dish, garnish with shredded leek and lemon wedges and serve with boiled rice or noodles.

COOK'S TIP

Insert the point of a sharp knife into the fish to test if it is cooked. The fish is cooked through if the knife goes into the flesh easily.

Mussels with Lemon Grass

Give fresh mussels a Far Eastern flavour by using some Kaffir lime leaves, garlic and lemon grass in the stock used for steaming them.

NUTRITIONAL INFORMATION

Calories 194	Sugar 0g
Protein 33g	Fat 7g
Carbohydrate 1g	Saturates 1g

10 MINS   10 MINS

SERVES 4

INGREDIENTS

750 g/1 lb 10 oz live mussels

1 tbsp sesame oil

3 shallots, chopped finely

2 garlic cloves, chopped finely

1 stalk lemon grass

2 Kaffir lime leaves

2 tbsp chopped fresh coriander (cilantro)

finely grated rind of 1 lime

2 tbsp lime juice

300 ml/½ pint/1¼ cups hot vegetable stock

crusty bread, to serve

fresh coriander (cilantro), to garnish

1 Using a small sharp knife, scrape the beards off the mussels under cold running water. Scrub them well, discarding any that are damaged or remain open when tapped. Keep rinsing until there is no trace of sand.

2 Heat the sesame oil in a large saucepan and fry the shallots and garlic gently until softened, about 2 minutes.

3 Bruise the lemon grass, using a meat mallet or rolling pin, and add to the pan with the Kaffir lime leaves, coriander (cilantro), lime rind and juice, mussels and stock. Put the lid on the saucepan and cook over a moderate heat for 3–5 minutes. Shake the pan from time to time.

4 Lift the mussels out into 4 warmed soup plates, discarding any that remain shut. Boil the remaining liquid rapidly to reduce slightly. Remove the lemon grass and lime leaves, then pour the liquid over the mussels.

5 Garnish with coriander (cilantro) and lime wedges, and serve at once.

COOK'S TIP

Mussels are now farmed, so they should be available from good fishmongers throughout the year.

Prawn (Shrimp) Stir-Fry

A very quick and tasty stir-fry using prawns (shrimp) and cucumber, cooked with lemon grass, chilli and ginger.

NUTRITIONAL INFORMATION

Calories ....178 Sugars 1g
Protein ....22g Fat 7g
Carbohydrate ....3g Saturates 1g

5 MINS   5 MINS

SERVES 4

I N G R E D I E N T S

½ cucumber

2 tbsp sunflower oil

6 spring onions (scallions), halved lengthways and cut into 4 cm/ 1½ inch lengths

1 stalk lemon grass, sliced thinly

1 garlic clove, chopped

1 tsp chopped fresh red chilli

125 g/4½ oz oyster mushrooms

1 tsp chopped ginger root

350 g/12 oz cooked peeled prawns (shrimp)

2 tsp cornflour (cornstarch)

2 tbsp water

1 tbsp dark soy sauce

½ tsp fish sauce

2 tbsp dry sherry or rice wine

boiled rice, to serve

1 Cut the cucumber into strips about 5 mm x 4 cm/¼ x 1¾ inches.

2 Heat the sunflower oil in a wok or large frying pan (skillet).

3 Add the spring onions (scallions), cucumber, lemon grass, garlic, chilli, oyster mushrooms and ginger to the wok or frying pan (skillet) and stir-fry for 2 minutes.

4 Add the prawns (shrimp) and stir-fry for a further minute.

5 Mix together the cornflour (cornstarch), water, soy sauce and fish sauce until smooth.

6 Stir the cornflour (cornstarch) mixture and sherry or wine into the wok and heat through, stirring, until the sauce has thickened. Serve with rice.

COOK'S TIP

The white part of the lemon grass stem can be thinly sliced and left in the cooked dish. If using the whole stem, remove it before serving. You can buy lemon grass chopped and dried, or preserved in jars, but neither has the fragrance or delicacy of the fresh variety.

Mullet with Ginger

Ginger is used widely in Chinese cooking for its strong, pungent flavour. Although fresh ginger is best, ground ginger may be used instead.

NUTRITIONAL INFORMATION

Calories 195	Sugars 6g
Protein 31g	Fat 3g
Carbohydrate 9g	Saturates 0g

  10 MINS   15 MINS

SERVES 4

I N G R E D I E N T S

1 whole mullet, cleaned and scaled

2 spring onions (scallions), chopped

1 tsp grated fresh root ginger

125 ml/4 fl oz/½ cup garlic wine vinegar

125 ml/4 fl oz/½ cup light soy sauce

3 tsp caster (superfine) sugar

dash of chilli sauce

125 ml/4 fl oz/½ cup fish stock

1 green (bell) pepper, seeded and thinly sliced

1 large tomato, skinned, seeded and cut into thin strips

salt and pepper

sliced tomato, to garnish

1 Rinse the fish inside and out and pat dry with kitchen paper (paper towels).

2 Make 3 diagonal slits in the flesh on each side of the fish. Season the fish with salt and pepper inside and out, according to taste.

3 Place the fish on a heatproof plate and scatter the chopped spring onions (scallions) and grated ginger over the top. Cover and steam for 10 minutes, or until the fish is cooked through.

4 Meanwhile, place the garlic wine vinegar, light soy sauce, caster (superfine) sugar, chilli sauce, fish stock, (bell) pepper and tomato in a saucepan and bring to the boil, stirring occasionally.

5 Cook the sauce over a high heat until the sauce has slightly reduced and thickened.

6 Remove the fish from the steamer and transfer to a warm serving dish. Pour the sauce over the fish, garnish with tomato slices and serve immediately.

VARIATION

Use fillets of fish for this recipe if preferred, and reduce the cooking time to 5–7 minutes.

Shrimp & Sweetcorn Patties

Chopped prawns (small shrimps) and sweetcorn are combined in a light batter, which is dropped into hot fat to make these tasty patties.

NUTRITIONAL INFORMATION

Calories	250	Sugars	.........1g
Protein	........17g	Fat	...........9g
Carbohydrate	...26g	Saturates	.......2g

35 MINS   20 MINS

SERVES 4

INGREDIENTS

125 g/4½ oz/1 cup plain (all-purpose) flour

1½ tsp baking powder

2 eggs

about 250 ml/9 fl oz/1 cup cold water

1 garlic clove, very finely chopped

3 spring onions (scallions), trimmed and very finely chopped

250 g/9 oz/1 cup peeled prawns (small shrimps), chopped

125 g/4½ oz/½ cup canned sweetcorn, drained

vegetable oil for frying

salt and pepper

TO GARNISH

spring onion (scallion) brushes

lime slices

1 chilli flower

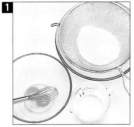

1 Sift the flour, baking powder and ½ tsp salt into a bowl. Add the eggs and half the water and beat to make a smooth batter, adding extra water to give the consistency of double (heavy) cream. Add the garlic and spring onions (scallions). Cover and leave for 30 minutes.

2 Stir the prawns (small shrimps) and corn into the batter. Season with pepper.

3 Heat 2–3 tablespoons of oil in a wok. Drop tablespoonfuls of the batter into the wok and cook over a medium heat until bubbles rise and the surface just sets. Flip the patties over and cook the other side until golden brown. Drain on kitchen paper (paper towels).

4 Cook the remaining batter in the same way, adding more oil to the wok if required. Garnish and serve at once.

COOK'S TIP

To make chilli flowers or spring onion (scallion) brushes hold the stem and cut down its length several times with a sharp knife. Place in a bowl of chilled water so that the 'petals' turn out. Remove the chilli seeds when the 'petals' have opened.

Fried Squid Flowers

The addition of green (bell) pepper and black bean sauce to the squid makes a colourful and delicious dish from the Cantonese school.

NUTRITIONAL INFORMATION

Calories 172	Sugars 1g	
Protein 13g	Fat 13g	
Carbohydrate 2g	Saturates 1g	

 10 MINS 5 MINS

SERVES 4

INGREDIENTS

350-400 g/12-14 oz prepared and cleaned squid (see Cook's Tip, below)

1 medium green (bell) pepper, cored and seeded

3-4 tbsp vegetable oil

1 garlic clove, finely chopped

¼ tsp finely chopped ginger root

2 tsp finely chopped spring onions (scallions)

½ tsp salt

2 tbsp crushed black bean sauce

1 tsp Chinese rice wine or dry sherry

a few drops sesame oil

boiled rice, to serve

1 If ready-prepared squid is not available, prepare as instructed in the Cook's Tip, below.

2 Open up the squid and, using a meat cleaver or sharp knife, score the inside of the flesh in a criss-cross pattern.

3 Cut the squid into pieces about the size of an oblong postage stamp.

4 Blanch the squid pieces in a bowl of boiling water for a few seconds. Remove and drain; dry well on absorbent kitchen paper (paper towels).

5 Cut the (bell) pepper into small triangular pieces. Heat the oil in a preheated wok or large frying pan (skillet) and stir-fry the (bell) pepper for about 1 minute.

6 Add the garlic, ginger, spring onion (scallion), salt and squid. Continue stirring for another minute.

7 Finally add the black bean sauce and Chinese rice wine or dry sherry, and blend well.

8 Transfer the squid flowers to a serving dish, sprinkle with sesame oil and serve with boiled rice.

COOK'S TIP

Clean the squid by first cutting off the head. Cut off the tentacles and reserve. Remove the small soft bone at the base of the tentacles and the transparent backbone, as well as the ink bag. Peel off the thin skin, then wash and dry well.

Scallop Pancakes

Scallops, like most shellfish require very little cooking, and this original dish is a perfect example of how to use shellfish to its full potential.

NUTRITIONAL INFORMATION

Calories ......240 Sugars 1g
Protein ....29g Fat 9g
Carbohydrate ....11g Saturates 1g

5 MINS   30 MINS

SERVES 4

I N G R E D I E N T S

100 g/3½ oz fine green beans

1 red chilli

450 g/1 lb scallops, without roe

1 egg

3 spring onions (scallions), sliced

50 g/1¾ oz/½ cup rice flour

1 tbsp fish sauce

oil, for frying

salt

sweet chilli dip, to serve

1 Using a sharp knife, trim the green beans and slice them very thinly.

2 Using a sharp knife, deseed and very finely chop the red chilli.

3 Bring a small saucepan of lightly salted water to the boil. Add the green beans to the pan and cook for 3–4 minutes or until just softened.

4 Roughly chop the scallops and place them in a large bowl. Add the cooked beans to the scallops.

5 Mix the egg with the spring onions (scallions), rice flour, fish sauce and chilli until well combined. Add to the scallops and mix well.

6 Heat about 2.5 cm/1 inch of oil in a large preheated wok. Add a ladleful of the mixture to the wok and cook for 5 minutes until golden and set.

7 Remove the pancake from the wok and leave to drain on absorbent kitchen paper (paper towels). Keep warm while cooking the remaining pancake mixture. Serve the pancakes hot with a sweet chilli dip.

VARIATION

You could use prawns (shrimp) or shelled clams instead of the scallops, if you prefer.

Sweet & Sour Cauliflower

Although sweet and sour flavourings are mainly associated with pork, they are ideal for flavouring vegetables as in this tasty recipe.

NUTRITIONAL INFORMATION

Calories 154   Sugars 16g
Protein . . . . .6g   Fat 7g
Carbohydrate . . .17g   Saturates 1g

5 MINS   20 MINS

SERVES 4

I N G R E D I E N T S

450 g/1 lb cauliflower florets

2 tbsp sunflower oil

1 onion, sliced

225 g/8 oz carrots, sliced

100 g/3½ oz mangetout (snow peas)

1 ripe mango, sliced

100 g/3½ oz/1 cup bean sprouts

3 tbsp chopped fresh coriander
(cilantro)

3 tbsp fresh lime juice

1 tbsp clear honey

6 tbsp coconut milk

1 Bring a large saucepan of water to the boil. Add the cauliflower to the pan and cook for 2 minutes. Drain the cauliflower thoroughly.

2 Heat the sunflower oil in a large preheated wok.

3 Add the onion and carrots to the wok and stir-fry for about 5 minutes.

4 Add the drained cauliflower and mangetout (snow peas) to the wok and stir-fry for 2–3 minutes.

5 Add the mango and bean sprouts to the wok and stir-fry for about 2 minutes.

6 Mix together the coriander (cilantro), lime juice, honey and coconut milk in a bowl.

7 Add the coriander (cilantro) and coconut mixture to the wok and stir-fry for about 2 minutes or until the juices are bubbling.

8 Transfer the sweet and sour cauliflower stir-fry to serving dishes and serve immediately.

VARIATION

Use broccoli instead of the cauliflower as an alternative, if you prefer.

Honey-Fried Chinese Leaves

Chinese leaves (cabbage) are rather similar to lettuce in that the leaves are delicate with a sweet flavour.

NUTRITIONAL INFORMATION

Calories 121	Sugars 6g	
Protein 5g	Fat 7g	
Carbohydrate . . .10g	Saturates 1g	

5 MINS   10 MINS

SERVES 4

I N G R E D I E N T S

450 g/1 lb Chinese leaves (cabbage)

1 tbsp peanut oil

1-cm/½-inch piece fresh root ginger, grated

2 garlic cloves, crushed

1 fresh red chilli, sliced

1 tbsp Chinese rice wine or dry sherry

4½ tsp light soy sauce

1 tbsp clear honey

125 ml/4 fl oz/½ cup orange juice

1 tbsp sesame oil

2 tsp sesame seeds

orange zest, to garnish

COOK'S TIP

Single-flower honey has a better, more individual flavour than blended honey. Acacia honey is typically Chinese, but you could also try clover, lemon blossom, lime flower or orange blossom.

1 Separate the Chinese leaves (cabbage) and shred them finely, using a sharp knife.

2 Heat the peanut oil in a preheated wok. Add the ginger, garlic and chilli to the wok and stir-fry the mixture for about 30 seconds.

3 Add the Chinese leaves (cabbage), Chinese rice wine or sherry, soy sauce, honey and orange juice to the wok. Reduce the heat and leave to simmer for 5 minutes.

4 Add the sesame oil to the wok, sprinkle the sesame seeds on top and mix to combine.

5 Transfer to a warm serving dish, garnish with the orange zest and serve immediately.

Spicy Aubergines (Eggplants)

Try to obtain the smaller Chinese aubergines (eggplants) for this dish, as they have a slightly sweeter taste.

NUTRITIONAL INFORMATION

Calories ....120 Sugars 7g
Protein ....2g Fat 9g
Carbohydrate ....9g Saturates 1g

35 MINS   20 MINS

SERVES 4

INGREDIENTS

450 g/1 lb aubergines (eggplants), rinsed

2 tsp salt

3 tbsp vegetable oil

2 garlic cloves, crushed

2.5-cm/1-inch piece fresh root ginger, chopped

1 onion, halved and sliced

1 fresh red chilli, sliced

2 tbsp dark soy sauce

1 tbsp hoisin sauce

½ tsp chilli sauce

1 tbsp dark brown sugar

1 tbsp wine vinegar

1 tsp ground Szechuan pepper

300 ml/½ pint/1¼ cups vegetable stock

1 Cut the aubergines (eggplants) into cubes if you are using the larger variety, or cut the smaller type in half. Place in a colander and sprinkle with the salt. Let stand for 30 minutes. Rinse under cold running water and pat dry with kitchen paper (paper towels).

2 Heat the oil in a preheated wok and add the garlic, ginger, onion and fresh chilli. Stir-fry for 30 seconds and add the aubergines (eggplants). Continue to cook for 1–2 minutes.

3 Add the soy sauce, hoisin sauce, chilli sauce, sugar, wine vinegar, Szechuan pepper and vegetable stock to the wok, reduce the heat and leave to simmer, uncovered, for 10 minutes, or until the aubergines (eggplants) are cooked.

4 Increase the heat and boil to reduce the sauce until thickened enough to coat the aubergines (eggplants). Serve immediately.

COOK'S TIP

Sprinkling the aubergines (eggplants) with salt and letting them stand removes the bitter juices, which would otherwise taint the flavour of the dish.

Lemon Chinese Leaves

These stir-fried Chinese leaves (cabbage) are served with a tangy sauce made of grated lemon rind, lemon juice and ginger.

NUTRITIONAL INFORMATION

Calories	120	Sugars	........0g
Protein	.........5g	Fat	..........8g
Carbohydrate	....8g	Saturates	.......1g

5 MINS   10 MINS

SERVES 4

I N G R E D I E N T S

500 g/1 lb 2 oz Chinese leaves (cabbage)

3 tbsp vegetable oil

1 cm/½ inch piece ginger root, grated

1 tsp salt

1 tsp sugar

125 ml/4 fl oz/½ cup water or vegetable stock

1 tsp grated lemon rind

1 tbsp cornflour (cornstarch)

1 tbsp lemon juice

1 Separate the Chinese leaves (cabbage), wash and drain thoroughly. Pat dry with absorbent kitchen paper (paper towels).

2 Cut the Chinese leaves (cabbage) into 5 cm/2 inch wide slices.

COOK'S TIP

If Chinese leaves (cabbage) are unavailable, substitute slices of savoy cabbage. Cook for 1 extra minute to soften the leaves.

3 Heat the oil in a wok and add the grated ginger root followed by the Chinese leaves (cabbage), stir-fry for 2–3 minutes or until the leaves begin to wilt.

4 Add the salt and sugar, and mix well until the leaves soften. Remove the leaves with a slotted spoon and set aside.

5 Add the water or stock to the wok with the lemon rind. Bring to the boil.

6 Meanwhile, mix the cornflour (cornstarch) to a smooth paste with the lemon juice, then add to the wok. Simmer, stirring constantly, for about 1 minute to make a smooth sauce.

7 Return the cooked Chinese leaves (cabbage) to the pan and mix thoroughly to coat the leaves in the sauce. Arrange on a serving plate and serve immediately.

Broccoli & Black Bean Sauce

Broccoli works well with the black bean sauce in this recipe, while the almonds add extra crunch and flavour.

NUTRITIONAL INFORMATION

Calories . . . . . . .139 Sugars 3g
Protein . . . . .7g Fat 10g
Carbohydrate . . . .5g Saturates 1g

  5 MINS   15 MINS

SERVES 4

I N G R E D I E N T S

450 g/1 lb broccoli florets

2 tbsp sunflower oil

1 onion, sliced

2 cloves garlic, thinly sliced

25 g/1 oz/¼ cup flaked (slivered) almonds

1 head Chinese leaves (cabbage), shredded

4 tbsp black bean sauce

1 Bring a large saucepan of water to the boil.

2 Add the broccoli florets to the pan and cook for 1 minute. Drain the broccoli thoroughly.

3 Meanwhile, heat the sunflower oil in a large preheated wok.

4 Add the onion and garlic slices to the wok and stir-fry until just beginning to brown.

5 Add the drained broccoli florets and the flaked (slivered) almonds to the mixture in the wok and stir-fry for a further 2–3 minutes.

6 Add the shredded Chinese leaves (cabbage) to the wok and stir-fry for a further 2 minutes, stirring the leaves briskly around the wok.

7 Stir the black bean sauce into the vegetables in the wok, tossing to coat the vegetables thoroughly in the sauce and cook until the juices are just beginning to bubble.

8 Transfer the vegetables to warm serving bowls and serve immediately.

VARIATION

Use unsalted cashew nuts instead of the almonds, if preferred.

Caraway Cabbage

This makes a delicious vegetable accompaniment to all types of food: it can also be served as a vegetarian main dish.

NUTRITIONAL INFORMATION

Calories 223	Sugars 17g
Protein 6g	Fat 14g
Carbohydrate ...18g	Saturates 1g

 5 MINS   10 MINS

SERVES 4

INGREDIENTS

500 g/1 lb 2 oz white cabbage

1 tbsp sunflower oil

4 spring onions (scallions), thinly sliced diagonally

60 g/2 oz/ 6 tbsp raisins

60 g/2 oz/½ cup walnut pieces or pecan nuts, roughly chopped

5 tbsp milk or vegetable stock

1 tbsp caraway seeds

1-2 tbsp freshly chopped mint

salt and pepper

mint sprigs, to garnish

1 Remove any outer leaves from the cabbage and cut out the stem, then shred the leaves very finely, either by hand or using the fine slicing blade on a food processor.

2 Heat the sunflower oil in a wok, swirling it around until it is really hot.

3 Add the spring onions (scallions) to the wok and stir-fry for a minute or so.

4 Add the shredded cabbage and stir-fry for 3-4 minutes, keeping the cabbage moving all the time and stirring from the outside to the centre of the wok. Make sure the cabbage does not stick to the wok or go brown.

5 Add the raisins, walnuts or pecans and milk or vegetable stock and continue to stir-fry for 3-4 minutes until the cabbage begins to soften slightly but is still crisp.

6 Season well with salt and pepper, add the caraway seeds and 1 tablespoon of the chopped mint and continue to stir-fry for a minute or so.

7 Serve sprinkled with the remaining chopped mint and garnish with sprigs of fresh mint.

VARIATION

Red cabbage may be cooked in the same way in the wok, but substitute 2 tablespoons red or white wine vinegar and 3 tablespoons water for the milk and add 1 tablespoon brown sugar. Add a finely chopped dessert apple if liked.

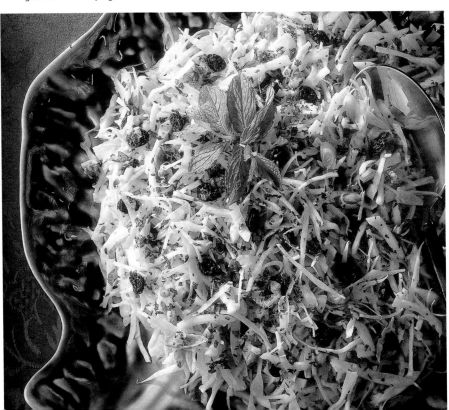

Deep-Fried Courgettes

These courgette (zucchini) fritters are irresistible and could be served as a starter or snack with a chilli dip.

NUTRITIONAL INFORMATION

Calories	117	Sugars	.........2g
Protein	.........3g	Fat	...........6g
Carbohydrate	...14g	Saturates	.......1g

5 MINS   20 MINS

SERVES 4

INGREDIENTS

450 g/1 lb courgettes (zucchini)

1 egg white

50 g/1¾ oz/⅓ cup cornflour (cornstarch)

1 tsp salt

1 tsp Chinese five-spice powder

oil, for deep-frying

chilli dip, to serve

1 Using a sharp knife, slice the courgettes (zucchini) into rings or chunky sticks.

2 Place the egg white in a small mixing bowl. Lightly whip the egg white until foamy, using a fork.

3 Mix the cornflour (cornstarch), salt and Chinese five-spice powder together and sprinkle on to a large plate.

4 Heat the oil for deep-frying in a large preheated wok or heavy-based frying pan (skillet).

5 Dip each piece of courgette (zucchini) into the beaten egg white then coat in the cornflour (cornstarch) and five-spice mixture.

6 Deep-fry the courgettes (zucchini), in batches, for about 5 minutes or until pale golden and crispy. Repeat with the remaining courgettes (zucchini).

7 Remove the courgettes (zucchini) with a slotted spoon and leave to drain on absorbent kitchen paper (paper towels) while deep-frying the remainder.

8 Transfer the courgettes (zucchini) to serving plates and serve immediately with a chilli dip.

VARIATION

Alter the seasoning by using chilli powder or curry powder instead of the Chinese five-spice powder, if you prefer.

Green & Black Bean Stir-Fry

A terrific side dish, the variety of greens in this recipe make it as attractive as it is tasty.

NUTRITIONAL INFORMATION

Calories	.88	Sugars	.2g
Protein	.2g	Fat	.7g
Carbohydrate	.4g	Saturates	.4g

 5 MINS   10 MINS

SERVES 4

I N G R E D I E N T S

225 g/8 oz fine green beans, sliced

4 shallots, sliced

100 g/3½ oz shiitake mushrooms, thinly sliced

1 clove garlic, crushed

1 Iceberg lettuce, shredded

1 tsp chilli oil

25 g/1 oz/2 tbsp butter

4 tbsp black bean sauce

1 Using a sharp knife, slice the fine green beans, shallots and shiitake mushrooms. Crush the garlic in a pestle and mortar and shred the Iceberg lettuce.

2 Heat the chilli oil and butter in a large preheated wok or frying pan (skillet).

3 Add the green beans, shallots, garlic and mushrooms to the wok and stir-fry for 2–3 minutes.

4 Add the shredded lettuce to the wok or frying pan (skillet) and stir-fry until the leaves have wilted.

5 Stir the black bean sauce into the mixture in the wok and heat through, tossing gently to mix, until the sauce is bubbling.

6 Transfer the green and black bean stir-fry to a warm serving dish and serve immediately.

COOK'S TIP

If possible, use Chinese green beans which are tender and can be eaten whole. They are available from specialist Chinese stores.

Bamboo with Spinach

In this recipe, spinach is fried with spices and then braised in a soy-flavoured sauce with bamboo shoots for a rich, delicious dish.

NUTRITIONAL INFORMATION

Calories 105	Sugars 1g	
Protein 3g	Fat 9g	
Carbohydrate 3g	Saturates 2g	

🧊 5 MINS   🕐 10 MINS

SERVES 4

INGREDIENTS

3 tbsp peanut oil

225 g/8 oz spinach, chopped

175 g/6 oz canned bamboo shoots, drained and rinsed

1 garlic clove, crushed

2 fresh red chillies, sliced

pinch of ground cinnamon

300 ml/½ pint/1¼ cups vegetable stock

pinch of sugar

pinch of salt

1 tbsp light soy sauce

COOK'S TIP

Fresh bamboo shoots are rarely available in the West and, in any case, are extremely time-consuming to prepare. Canned bamboo shoots are quite satisfactory, as they are used to provide a crunchy texture, rather than for their flavour, which is fairly insipid.

1 Heat the peanut oil in a preheated wok or large frying pan (skillet), swirling the oil around the base of the wok until it is really hot.

2 Add the spinach and bamboo shoots to the wok and stir-fry for 1 minute.

3 Add the garlic, chillies and cinnamon to the mixture in the wok and stir-fry for a further 30 seconds.

4 Stir in the stock, sugar, salt and light soy sauce, cover and cook over a medium heat for 5 minutes, or until the vegetables are cooked through and the sauce has reduced. If there is too much cooking liquid, blend a little cornflour (cornstarch) with double the quantity of cold water and stir into the sauce.

5 Transfer the bamboo shoots and spinach to a serving dish and serve.

Vegetable Chop Suey

Make sure that the vegetables are all cut into pieces of a similar size in this recipe, so that they cook within the same amount of time.

NUTRITIONAL INFORMATION

Calories ....155 Sugars 6g
Protein ....4g Fat 12g
Carbohydrate ....9g Saturates 2g

5 MINS   5 MINS

SERVES 4

INGREDIENTS

1 yellow (bell) pepper, seeded

1 red (bell) pepper, seeded

1 carrot

1 courgette (zucchini)

1 fennel bulb

1 onion

60 g/2 oz mangetout (snow peas)

2 tbsp peanut oil

3 garlic cloves, crushed

1 tsp grated fresh root ginger

125 g/4½ oz bean sprouts

2 tsp light brown sugar

2 tbsp light soy sauce

125 ml/4 fl oz/½ cup vegetable stock

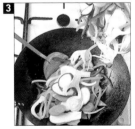

1 Cut the (bell) peppers, carrot, courgette (zucchini) and fennel into thin slices. Cut the onion into quarters and then cut each quarter in half. Slice the mangetout (snow peas) diagonally to create the maximum surface area.

2 Heat the oil in a preheated wok, add the garlic and ginger and stir-fry for 30 seconds. Add the onion and stir-fry for a further 30 seconds.

3 Add the (bell) peppers, carrot, courgette (zucchini), fennel and mangetout (snow peas) to the wok and stir-fry for 2 minutes.

4 Add the bean sprouts to the wok and stir in the sugar, soy sauce and stock. Reduce the heat to low and simmer for 1–2 minutes, until the vegetables are tender and coated in the sauce.

5 Transfer the vegetables and sauce to a serving dish and serve immediately.

VARIATION

Use any combination of colourful vegetables that you have to hand to make this versatile dish.

Tofu with Mushrooms

Chunks of cucumber and smoked tofu (bean curd) stir-fried with straw mushrooms, mangetout (snow peas) and corn in a yellow bean sauce.

NUTRITIONAL INFORMATION

Calories	130	Sugars	.........2g
Protein	.........9g	Fat	..........9g
Carbohydrate	....3g	Saturates	.......1g

 15 MINS   10 MINS

SERVES 4

INGREDIENTS

1 large cucumber

1 tsp salt

225 g/8 oz smoked tofu (bean curd)

2 tbsp vegetable oil

60 g/2 oz mangetout (snow peas)

125 g/4½ oz/8 baby corn

1 celery stick, sliced diagonally

425 g/15 oz can straw mushrooms,
   drained

2 spring onions (scallions),
   cut into strips

1 cm/½ inch piece ginger root, chopped

1 tbsp yellow bean sauce

1 tbsp light soy sauce

1 tbsp dry sherry

1 Halve the cucumber lengthways and remove the seeds, using a teaspoon or melon baller.

2 Cut the cucumber into cubes, place in a colander and sprinkle over the salt. Leave to drain for 10 minutes. Rinse thoroughly in cold water to remove the salt and drain thoroughly on absorbent kitchen paper (paper towels).

3 Cut the tofu (bean curd) into cubes.

4 Heat the vegetable oil in a wok or large frying pan (skillet) until smoking.

5 Add the tofu (bean curd), mangetout (snow peas), baby corn and celery to the wok. Stir until the tofu (bean curd) is lightly browned.

6 Add the straw mushrooms, spring onions (scallions) and ginger, and stir-fry for a further minute.

7 Stir in the cucumber, yellow bean sauce, light soy sauce, dry sherry and 2 tablespoons of water. Stir-fry for 1 minute and ensure that all the vegetables are coated in the sauces before serving.

COOK'S TIP

Straw mushrooms are available in cans from oriental suppliers and some supermarkets. If unavailable, substitute 250 g/ 9 oz baby button mushrooms.

Tofu with Hot & Sweet Sauce

Golden pieces of tofu (bean curd) are served in a hot and creamy peanut and chilli sauce for a classic vegetarian starter.

NUTRITIONAL INFORMATION

Calories	367	Sugars	.........5g
Protein	........18g	Fat	..........30g
Carbohydrate	....8g	Saturates	.......5g

 5 MINS 15 MINS

SERVES 4

INGREDIENTS

450 g/1 lb tofu (bean curd), cubed

oil, for frying

SAUCE

6 tbsp crunchy peanut butter

1 tbsp sweet chilli sauce

150 ml/¼ pint/⅔ cup coconut milk

1 tbsp tomato purée (paste)

25 g/1 oz/¼ cup chopped salted peanuts

1 Pat away any moisture from the tofu (bean curd), using absorbent kitchen paper (paper towels).

2 Heat the oil in a large wok or frying pan (skillet) until very hot.

3 Add the tofu (bean curd) to the wok and cook, in batches, for about 5 minutes, or until golden and crispy.

4 Remove the tofu (bean curd) with a slotted spoon, transfer to absorbent kitchen paper (paper towels) and leave to drain.

5 To make the peanut and chilli sauce, mix together the crunchy peanut butter, sweet chilli sauce, coconut milk, tomato purée (paste) and chopped salted peanuts in a bowl. Add a little boiling water if necessary to achieve a smooth consistency. Stir well until the ingredients are thoroughly blended.

6 Transfer the tofu (bean curd) to serving plates and pour the sauce over the top. Alternatively, pour the sauce into a serving dish and serve separately.

COOK'S TIP

Make sure that all of the moisture has been absorbed from the tofu (bean curd) before frying, otherwise it will not crispen.

Cook the peanut and chilli sauce in a saucepan over a gentle heat before serving, if you prefer.

Tofu Casserole

Tofu (bean curd) is ideal for absorbing all the other flavours in this dish. If marinated tofu (bean curd) is used, it will add a flavour of its own.

NUTRITIONAL INFORMATION

Calories	228	Sugars	.........3g
Protein	........16g	Fat	..........15g
Carbohydrate	....7g	Saturates	.......2g

 5 MINS   15 MINS

SERVES 4

I N G R E D I E N T S

450 g/1 lb tofu (bean curd)

2 tbsp peanut oil

8 spring onions (scallions), cut into batons

2 celery sticks, sliced

125 g/4½ oz broccoli florets

125 g/4½ oz courgettes (zucchini), sliced

2 garlic cloves, thinly sliced

450 g/1 lb baby spinach

rice, to serve

S A U C E

425 ml/¾ pint/2 cups vegetable stock

2 tbsp light soy sauce

3 tbsp hoisin sauce

½ tsp chilli powder

1 tbsp sesame oil

1 Cut the tofu (bean curd) into 2.5-cm/1-inch cubes and set aside until required.

2 Heat the peanut oil in a preheated wok or large frying pan (skillet).

3 Add the spring onions (scallions), celery, broccoli, courgettes (zucchini), garlic, spinach and tofu (bean curd) to the wok or frying pan (skillet) and stir-fry for 3–4 minutes.

4 To make the sauce, mix together the vegetable stock, soy sauce, hoisin sauce, chilli powder and sesame oil in a flameproof casserole and bring to the boil.

5 Add the stir-fried vegetables and tofu (bean curd) to the saucepan, reduce the heat, cover and simmer for 10 minutes.

6 Transfer the tofu (bean curd) and vegetables to a warm serving dish and serve with rice.

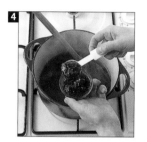

VARIATION

This recipe has a green vegetable theme, but alter the colour and flavour by adding your favourite vegetables. Add 75 g/2¾ oz fresh or canned and drained straw mushrooms with the vegetables in step 2.

Tofu with (Bell) Peppers

Tofu (bean curd) is perfect for marinating as it readily absorbs flavours for a great tasting main dish.

NUTRITIONAL INFORMATION

Calories 267	Sugars 2g
Protein 9g	Fat 23g
Carbohydrate 5g	Saturates 3g

25 MINS   15 MINS

SERVES 4

INGREDIENTS

350 g/12 oz tofu (bean curd)

2 cloves garlic, crushed

4 tbsp soy sauce

1 tbsp sweet chilli sauce

6 tbsp sunflower oil

1 onion, sliced

1 green (bell) pepper, deseeded
and diced

1 tbsp sesame oil

1 Using a sharp knife, cut the tofu (bean curd) into bite-sized pieces. Place the tofu (bean curd) in a shallow non-metallic dish.

2 Mix together the garlic, soy sauce and sweet chilli sauce and drizzle over the tofu (bean curd). Toss well to coat and leave to marinate for about 20 minutes.

3 Meanwhile, heat the sunflower oil in a large preheated wok.

4 Add the onion to the wok and stir-fry over a high heat until brown and crispy. Remove the onion with a slotted spoon and leave to drain on absorbent kitchen paper (paper towels).

5 Add the tofu (bean curd) to the hot oil and stir-fry for about 5 minutes.

6 Remove all but 1 tablespoon of the sunflower oil from the wok. Add the (bell) pepper to the wok and stir-fry for 2–3 minutes, or until softened.

7 Return the tofu (bean curd) and onions to the wok and heat through, stirring occasionally.

8 Drizzle with sesame oil. Transfer to serving plates and serve immediately.

COOK'S TIP

If you are in a real hurry, buy ready-marinated tofu (bean curd) from your supermarket.

Egg Fried Rice

In this classic Chinese dish, boiled rice is fried with peas, spring onions (scallions) and egg and flavoured with soy sauce.

NUTRITIONAL INFORMATION

Calories 203	Sugars 1g	
Protein 9g	Fat 11g	
Carbohydrate ...19g	Saturates 2g	

20 MINS   10 MINS

SERVES 4

INGREDIENTS

150 g/5½ oz/⅔ cup long-grain rice

3 eggs, beaten

2 tbsp vegetable oil

2 garlic cloves, crushed

4 spring onions (scallions), chopped

125 g/4½oz/1 cup cooked peas

1 tbsp light soy sauce

pinch of salt

shredded spring onion (scallion),
  to garnish

1 Cook the rice in a pan of boiling water for 10-12 minutes, until almost cooked, but not soft. Drain well, rinse under cold water and drain again.

2 Place the beaten eggs in a saucepan and cook over a gentle heat, stirring until softly scrambled.

3 Heat the vegetable oil in a preheated wok or large frying pan (skillet), swirling the oil around the base of the wok until it is really hot.

4 Add the crushed garlic, spring onions (scallions) and peas and sauté, stirring occasionally, for 1-2 minutes. Stir the rice into the wok, mixing to combine.

5 Add the eggs, light soy sauce and a pinch of salt to the wok or frying pan (skillet) and stir to mix the egg in thoroughly.

6 Transfer the egg fried rice to serving dishes and serve garnished with the shredded spring onion (scallion).

COOK'S TIP

The rice is rinsed under cold water to wash out the starch and prevent it from sticking together.

Chatuchak Fried Rice

An excellent way to use up leftover rice. Pop it in the freezer as soon as it is cool, and it will be ready to reheat at any time.

NUTRITIONAL INFORMATION

Calories	241	Sugars	.........5g
Protein	.........7g	Fat	...........5g
Carbohydrate	...46g	Saturates	.......1g

25 MINS   15 MINS

SERVES 4

I N G R E D I E N T S

1 tbsp sunflower oil

3 shallots, chopped finely

2 garlic cloves, crushed

1 red chilli, deseeded and chopped finely

2.5-cm/1-inch piece ginger root, shredded finely

½ green (bell) pepper, deseeded and sliced fincly

150 g/5½ oz/2-3 baby aubergines (eggplants), quartered

90 g/3 oz sugar snap peas or mangetout (snow peas), trimmed and blanched

90 g/3 oz/6 baby sweetcorn, halved lengthways and blanched

1 tomato, cut into 8 pieces

90 g/3 oz/1½ cups bean sprouts

500 g/1 lb 2 oz/3 cups cooked jasmine rice

2 tbsp tomato ketchup

2 tbsp light soy sauce

TO GARNISH

fresh coriander (cilantro) leaves

lime wedges

1 Heat the sunflower oil in a wok or large, heavy frying pan (skillet) over a high heat.

2 Add the shallots, garlic, chilli and ginger to the wok or frying pan (skillet). Stir until the shallots have softened.

3 Add the green (bell) pepper and baby aubergines (eggplants) and stir well.

4 Add the sugar snap peas or mangetout (snow peas), baby sweetcorn, tomato and bean sprouts. Stir-fry for 3 minutes.

5 Add the cooked jasmine rice to the wok, and lift and stir with two spoons for 4–5 minutes, until no more steam is released.

6 Stir the tomato ketchup and soy sauce into the mixture in the wok.

7 Serve the Chatuchak fried rice immediately, garnished with coriander (cilantro) leaves and lime wedges to squeeze over.

Green-Fried Rice

Spinach is used in this recipe to give the rice a wonderful green colouring. Tossed with the carrot strips, it is a really appealing dish.

NUTRITIONAL INFORMATION

Calories 139	Sugars 2g	
Protein 3g	Fat 7g	
Carbohydrate . . .18g	Saturates 1g	

5 MINS   20 MINS

SERVES 4

INGREDIENTS

150 g/5½ oz/⅔ cup long-grain rice

2 tbsp vegetable oil

2 garlic cloves, crushed

1 tsp grated fresh root ginger

1 carrot, cut into matchsticks

1 courgette (zucchini), diced

225 g/8 oz baby spinach

2 tsp light soy sauce

2 tsp light brown sugar

1 Cook the rice in a saucepan of boiling water for about 15 minutes. Drain the rice well, rinse under cold running water and then rinse the rice thoroughly again. Set aside until required.

2 Heat the vegetable oil in a preheated wok or large, heavy-based frying pan (skillet).

3 Add the crushed garlic and grated fresh root ginger to the wok or frying pan (skillet) and stir-fry for about 30 seconds.

4 Add the carrot matchsticks and diced courgette (zucchini) to the mixture in the wok and stir-fry for about 2 minutes, so the vegetables still retain their crunch.

5 Add the baby spinach and stir-fry for 1 minute, until wilted.

6 Add the rice, soy sauce and sugar to the wok and mix together well.

7 Transfer the green-fried rice to serving dishes and serve immediately.

COOK'S TIP

Light soy sauce has more flavour than the sweeter, dark soy sauce, which gives the food a rich, reddish colour.

Vegetable Fried Rice

This dish can be served as part of a substantial meal for a number of people or as a vegetarian meal in itself for four.

NUTRITIONAL INFORMATION

Calories 175   Sugars 3g
Protein . . . . .3g   Fat 10g
Carbohydrate . . .20g   Saturates 2g

 10 MINS   20 MINS

SERVES 4

I N G R E D I E N T S

125 g/4½ oz/⅔ cup long-grain white rice

3 tbsp peanut oil

2 garlic cloves, crushed

½ tsp Chinese five-spice powder

60 g/2 oz/⅓ cup green beans

1 green (bell) pepper, seeded and chopped

4 baby corn cobs, sliced

25 g/1 oz bamboo shoots, chopped

3 tomatoes, skinned, seeded and chopped

60 g/2 oz/½ cup cooked peas

1 tsp sesame oil

1 Bring a large saucepan of water to the boil.

2 Add the long-grain white rice to the saucepan and cook for about 15 minutes. Drain the rice well, rinse under cold running water and drain thoroughly again.

3 Heat the peanut oil in a preheated wok or large frying pan (skillet). Add the garlic and Chinese five-spice and stir-fry for 30 seconds.

4 Add the green beans, chopped green (bell) pepper and sliced corn cobs and stir-fry the ingredients in the wok for 2 minutes.

5 Stir the bamboo shoots, tomatoes, peas and rice into the mixture in the wok and stir-fry for 1 further minute.

6 Sprinkle with sesame oil and transfer to serving dishes. Serve immediately.

VARIATION

Use a selection of vegetables of your choice in this recipe, cutting them to a similar size in order to ensure that they cook in the same amount of time.

Chinese Risotto

Risotto is a creamy Italian dish made with arborio or risotto rice. This Chinese version is simply delicious!

NUTRITIONAL INFORMATION

Calories	436	Sugars	.........7g
Protein	.......13g	Fat	..........14g
Carbohydrate	...70g	Saturates	.......4g

 5 MINS   25 MINS

SERVES 4

INGREDIENTS

2 tbsp groundnut oil

1 onion, sliced

2 cloves garlic, crushed

1 tsp Chinese five-spice powder

225 g/8 oz Chinese sausage, sliced

225 g/8 oz carrots, diced

1 green (bell) pepper, deseeded and diced

275 g/9½oz/1⅓ cups risotto rice

850 ml/1½ pints/1¾ cups vegetable or chicken stock

1 tbsp fresh chives

1 Heat the groundnut oil in a large preheated wok or heavy-based frying pan (skillet).

2 Add the onion slices, crushed garlic and Chinese five spice powder to the wok or frying pan (skillet) and stir-fry for 1 minute.

3 Add the Chinese sausage, carrots and green (bell) pepper to the wok and stir to combine.

4 Stir in the risotto rice and cook for 1 minute.

5 Gradually add the vegetable or chicken stock, a little at a time, stirring constantly until the liquid has been completely absorbed and the rice grains are tender.

6 Snip the chives with a pair of clean kitchen scissors and stir into the wok with the last of the stock.

7 Transfer the Chinese risotto to warm serving bowls and serve immediately.

COOK'S TIP

Chinese sausage is highly flavoured and is made from chopped pork fat, pork meat and spices. Use a spicy Portuguese sausage if Chinese sausage is unavailable.

Chicken Chow Mein

This classic dish requires no introduction as it is already a favourite amongst most Chinese food-eaters.

NUTRITIONAL INFORMATION

Calories 230   Sugars 2g
Protein . . . . .19g   Fat 11g
Carbohydrate . . .14g   Saturates 2g

5 MINS   20 MINS

SERVES 4

INGREDIENTS

250 g/9 oz packet medium egg noodles

2 tbsp sunflower oil

275 g/9½ oz cooked chicken breasts, shredded

1 clove garlic, finely chopped

1 red (bell) pepper, deseeded and thinly sliced

100 g/3½ oz shiitake mushrooms, sliced

6 spring onions (scallions), sliced

100 g/3½ oz/1 cup bean sprouts

3 tbsp soy sauce

1 tbsp sesame oil

1 Place the egg noodles in a large bowl or dish and break them up slightly. Pour over enough boiling water to cover the noodles and leave to stand.

2 Heat the sunflower oil in a large preheated wok. Add the shredded chicken, finely chopped garlic, (bell) pepper slices, mushrooms, spring onions (scallions) and bean sprouts to the wok and stir-fry for about 5 minutes.

3 Drain the noodles thoroughly. Add the noodles to the wok, toss well and stir-fry for a further 5 minutes.

4 Drizzle the soy sauce and sesame oil over the chow mein and toss until well combined.

5 Transfer the chicken chow mein to warm serving bowls and serve immediately.

VARIATION

You can make the chow mein with a selection of vegetables for a vegetarian dish, if you prefer.

Cantonese Fried Noodles

This dish is usually served as a snack or light meal. It may also be served as an accompaniment to plain meat and fish dishes.

NUTRITIONAL INFORMATION

Calories 385	Sugars 6g
Protein 38g	Fat 17g
Carbohydrate . . .21g	Saturates 4g

🥔 5 MINS   🕐 15 MINS

SERVES 4

I N G R E D I E N T S

350 g/12 oz egg noodles

3 tbsp vegetable oil

675 g/1½ lb lean beef steak, cut into thin strips

125 g/4½ oz green cabbage, shredded

75 g/2¾ oz bamboo shoots

6 spring onions (scallions), sliced

25 g/1 oz green beans, halved

1 tbsp dark soy sauce

2 tbsp beef stock

1 tbsp dry sherry

1 tbsp light brown sugar

2 tbsp chopped parsley, to garnish

1 Cook the noodles in a saucepan of boiling water for 2-3 minutes. Drain well, rinse under cold running water and drain thoroughly again.

2 Heat 1 tablespoon of the oil in a preheated wok or frying pan (skillet), swirling it around until it is really hot

3 Add the noodles and stir-fry for 1-2 minutes. Drain the noodles and set aside until required.

4 Heat the remaining oil in the wok. Add the beef and stir-fry for 2-3 minutes. Add the cabbage, bamboo shoots, spring onions (scallions) and beans to the wok and stir-fry for 1-2 minutes.

5 Add the soy sauce, beef stock, dry sherry and light brown sugar to the wok, stirring to mix well.

6 Stir the noodles into the mixture in the wok, tossing to mix well. Transfer to serving bowls, garnish with chopped parsley and serve immediately.

VARIATION

You can vary the vegetables in this dish depending on seasonal availability or whatever you have at hand – try broccoli, green (bell) pepper or spinach.

Lamb with Noodles

Lamb is quick fried, coated in a soy sauce and served on a bed of transparent noodles for a richly flavoured dish.

NUTRITIONAL INFORMATION

Calories ....285 Sugars 1g
Protein ....27g Fat 16g
Carbohydrate ...10g Saturates 6g

5 MINS   15 MINS

SERVES 4

I N G R E D I E N T S

150 g/5½ oz cellophane noodles

2 tbsp peanut oil

450 g/1 lb lean lamb, thinly sliced

2 garlic cloves, crushed

2 leeks, sliced

3 tbsp dark soy sauce

250 ml/9 fl oz/1 cup lamb stock

dash of chilli sauce

red chilli strips, to garnish

1 Bring a large saucepan of water to the boil. Add the cellophane noodles and cook for 1 minute. Drain the noodles well, place in a sieve, rinse under cold running water and drain thoroughly again. Set aside until required.

2 Heat the peanut oil in a preheated wok or frying pan (skillet), swirling the oil around until it is really hot.

3 Add the lamb to the wok or frying pan (skillet) and stir-fry for about 2 minutes.

4 Add the crushed garlic and sliced leeks to the wok and stir-fry for a further 2 minutes.

5 Stir in the dark soy sauce, lamb stock and chilli sauce and cook for 3-4

minutes, stirring frequently, until the meat is cooked through.

6 Add the drained cellophane noodles to the wok or frying pan (skillet) and cook for about 1 minute, stirring, until heated through.

7 Transfer the lamb and cellophane noodles to serving plates, garnish with red chilli strips and serve.

COOK'S TIP

Transparent noodles are available in Chinese supermarkets. Use egg noodles instead if transparent noodles are unavailable, and cook them according to the instructions on the packet.

Pork Chow Mein

This is a basic recipe – the meat and/or vegetables can be varied as much as you like.

NUTRITIONAL INFORMATION

Calories 239	Sugars 1g
Protein 17g	Fat 14g
Carbohydrate ...12g	Saturates 2g

 15 MINS   15 MINS

SERVES 4

INGREDIENTS

250 g/9 oz egg noodles

4-5 tbsp vegetable oil

250 g/9 oz pork fillet, cooked

125g/4½ oz French (green) beans

2 tbsp light soy sauce

1 tsp salt

½ tsp sugar

1 tbsp Chinese rice wine or dry sherry

2 spring onions (scallions), finely shredded

a few drops sesame oil

chilli sauce, to serve (optional)

1 Cook the noodles in boiling water according to the instructions on the packet, then drain and rinse under cold water. Drain again then toss with 1 tablespoon of the oil.

2 Slice the pork into thin shreds and top and tail the beans.

3 Heat 3 tablespoons of oil in a preheated wok until hot. Add the noodles and stir-fry for 2-3 minutes with 1 tablespoon soy sauce, then remove to a serving dish. Keep warm.

4 Heat the remaining oil and stir-fry the beans and meat for 2 minutes. Add the salt, sugar, wine or sherry, the

remaining soy sauce and about half the spring onions (scallions) to the wok.

5 Stir the mixture in the wok, adding a little stock if necessary, then pour on top of the noodles, and sprinkle with sesame oil and the remaining spring onions (scallions).

6 Serve the chow mein hot or cold with chilli sauce, if desired.

COOK'S TIP

Chow Mein literally means 'stir-fried noodles' and is highly popular in the West as well as in China. Almost any ingredient can be added, such as fish, meat, poultry or vegetables. It is very popular for lunch and makes a tasty salad served cold.

Oyster Sauce Noodles

Chicken and noodles are cooked and then tossed in an oyster sauce and egg mixture in this delicious recipe.

NUTRITIONAL INFORMATION

Calories 278   Sugars 2g
Protein ....30g   Fat 12g
Carbohydrate ...13g   Saturates 3g

5 MINS   25 MINS

SERVES 4

I N G R E D I E N T S

250 g/9 oz egg noodles

450 g/1 lb chicken thighs

2 tbsp groundnut oil

100 g/3½ oz carrots, sliced

3 tbsp oyster sauce

2 eggs

3 tbsp cold water

1 Place the egg noodles in a large bowl or dish. Pour enough boiling water over the noodles to cover and leave to stand for 10 minutes.

2 Meanwhile, remove the skin from the chicken thighs. Cut the chicken flesh into small pieces, using a sharp knife.

VARIATION

Flavour the eggs with soy sauce or hoisin sauce as an alternative to the oyster sauce, if you prefer.

 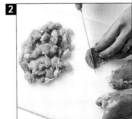 

3 Heat the groundnut oil in a large preheated wok or frying pan (skillet), swirling the oil around the base of the wok until it is really hot.

4 Add the pieces of chicken and the carrot slices to the wok and stir-fry for about 5 minutes.

5 Drain the noodles thoroughly. Add the noodles to the wok and stir-fry for a

further 2–3 minutes or until the noodles are heated through.

6 Beat together the oyster sauce, eggs and 3 tablespoons of cold water. Drizzle the mixture over the noodles and stir-fry for a further 2–3 minutes or until the eggs set.

7 Transfer the mixture in the wok to warm serving bowls and serve hot.

Noodles with Chilli & Prawn

This is a simple dish to prepare and is packed with flavour, making it an ideal choice for special occasions.

NUTRITIONAL INFORMATION

Calories 259	Sugars 9g
Protein 28g	Fat 8g
Carbohydrate ...20g	Saturates 1g

10 MINS   5 MINS

SERVES 4

I N G R E D I E N T S

250 g/9 oz thin glass noodles

2 tbsp sunflower oil

1 onion, sliced

2 red chillies, deseeded and very finely chopped

4 lime leaves, thinly shredded

1 tbsp fresh coriander (cilantro)

2 tbsp palm or caster (superfine) sugar

2 tbsp fish sauce

450 g/1 lb raw tiger prawns (jumbo shrimp), peeled

1 Place the noodles in a large bowl. Pour over enough boiling water to cover the noodles and leave to stand for 5 minutes. Drain thoroughly and set aside until required.

COOK'S TIP

If you cannot buy raw tiger prawns (jumbo shrimp), use cooked prawns (shrimp) instead and cook them with the noodles for 1 minute only, just to heat through.

2 Heat the sunflower oil in a large preheated wok or frying pan (skillet) until it is really hot.

3 Add the onion, red chillies and lime leaves to the wok and stir-fry for 1 minute.

4 Add the coriander (cilantro), palm or caster (superfine) sugar, fish sauce and prawns (shrimp) to the wok or frying pan (skillet) and stir-fry for a further 2 minutes or until the prawns (shrimp) turn pink.

5 Add the drained noodles to the wok, toss to mix well, and stir-fry for 1–2 minutes or until heated through.

6 Transfer the noodles and prawns (shrimp) to warm serving bowls and serve immediately.

Noodles with Prawns (Shrimp)

This is a simple dish using egg noodles and large prawns (shrimp), which give the dish a wonderful flavour, texture and colour.

NUTRITIONAL INFORMATION

Calories 142	Sugars 0.4g
Protein 11g	Fat 7g
Carbohydrate 11g	Saturates 1g

 5 MINS   10 MINS

SERVES 4

I N G R E D I E N T S

225 g/8 oz thin egg noodles

2 tbsp peanut oil

1 garlic clove, crushed

½ tsp ground star anise

1 bunch spring onions (scallions), cut into 5-cm/2-inch pieces

24 raw tiger prawns (jumbo shrimp), peeled with tails intact

2 tbsp light soy sauce

2 tsp lime juice

lime wedges, to garnish

1 Blanch the noodles in a saucepan of boiling water for about 2 minutes.

2 Drain the noodles well, rinse under cold water and drain thoroughly again. Keep warm and set aside until required.

3 Heat the peanut oil in a preheated wok or large frying pan (skillet) until almost smoking.

4 Add the crushed garlic and ground star anise to the wok and stir-fry for 30 seconds.

5 Add the spring onions (scallions) and tiger prawns (jumbo shrimp) to the wok and stir-fry for 2-3 minutes.

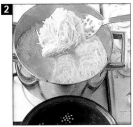  

6 Stir in the light soy sauce, lime juice and noodles and mix well.

7 Cook the mixture in the wok for about 1 minute until thoroughly heated through and all the ingredients are thoroughly incorporated.

8 Spoon the noodle and prawn mixture into a warm serving dish. Transfer to serving bowls, garnish with lime wedges and serve immediately.

COOK'S TIP

If fresh egg noodles are available, these require very little cooking: simply place in boiling water for about 3 minutes, then drain and toss in oil. Noodles can be boiled and eaten plain, or stir-fried with meat and vegetables for a light meal or snack.

Chicken & Noodle One-Pot

Flavoursome chicken and vegetables cooked with Chinese egg noodles in a coconut sauce. Serve in deep soup bowls.

NUTRITIONAL INFORMATION

Calories	256	Sugars	.........7g
Protein	........30g	Fat	...........8g
Carbohydrate	...18g	Saturates	.......2g

 5 MINS   20 MINS

SERVES 4

I N G R E D I E N T S

1 tbsp sunflower oil

1 onion, sliced

1 garlic clove, crushed

2.5 cm/1 inch root ginger, peeled and grated

1 bunch spring onions (scallions), sliced diagonally

500 g/1 lb 2 oz chicken breast fillet, skinned and cut into bite-sized pieces

2 tbsp mild curry paste

450 ml/16 fl oz/2 cups coconut milk

300 ml/½ pint/1¼ cups chicken stock

250 g/9 oz Chinese egg noodles

2 tsp lime juice

salt and pepper

basil sprigs, to garnish

1 Heat the sunflower oil in a wok or large, heavy-based frying pan (skillet).

2 Add the onion, garlic, ginger and spring onions (scallions) to the wok and stir-fry for 2 minutes until softened.

3 Add the chicken and curry paste and stir-fry for 4 minutes, or until the vegetables and chicken are golden brown. Stir in the coconut milk, stock and salt and pepper to taste, and mix well.

4 Bring to the boil, break the noodles into large pieces, if necessary, add to the pan, cover and simmer for about 6-8 minutes until the noodles are just tender, stirring occasionally.

5 Add the lime juice and adjust the seasoning, if necessary.

6 Serve the chicken and noodle one-pot at once in deep soup bowls, garnished with basil sprigs.

COOK'S TIP

If you enjoy hot flavours, substitute the mild curry paste in the above recipe with hot curry paste (found in most supermarkets) but reduce the quantity to 1 tablespoon.

Sweet Fruit Wontons

These sweet wontons are very adaptable and may be filled with whole, small fruits or a spicy chopped mixture as here.

10 MINS   15 MINS

SERVES 4

I N G R E D I E N T S

12 wonton wrappers

2 tsp cornflour (cornstarch)

6 tsp cold water

oil, for deep-frying

2 tbsp clear honey

selection of fresh fruit (such as kiwi fruit, limes, oranges, mango and apples), sliced, to serve

F I L L I N G

175 g/6 oz/1 cup chopped dried, stoned (pitted) dates

2 tsp dark brown sugar

½ tsp ground cinnamon

1 To make the filling, mix together the dates, sugar and cinnamon in a bowl.

2 Spread out the wonton wrappers on a chopping board and spoon a little of the filling into the centre of each wrapper.

  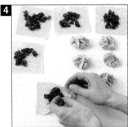

3 Blend the cornflour (cornstarch) and water and brush this mixture around the edges of the wrappers.

4 Fold the wrappers over the filling, bringing the edges together, then bring the two corners together, sealing with the cornflour (cornstarch) mixture.

5 Heat the oil for deep-frying in a wok to 180°C/350°F, or until a cube of bread browns in 30 seconds. Fry the wontons, in batches, for 2-3 minutes, until golden. Remove the wontons from the oil with a slotted spoon and leave to drain on absorbent kitchen paper (paper towels).

6 Place the honey in a bowl and stand it in warm water, to soften it slightly. Drizzle the honey over the sweet fruit wontons and serve with a selection of fresh fruit.

COOK'S TIP

Wonton wrappers may be found in Chinese supermarkets.

Exotic Fruit Salad

This is a sophisticated fruit salad that makes use of some of the exotic fruits that can now be seen in the supermarket.

NUTRITIONAL INFORMATION

Calories 149   Sugars 39g
Protein ....1g   Fat 0.1g
Carbohydrate ...39g   Saturates 0g

10 MINS   15 MINS

SERVES 6

I N G R E D I E N T S

3 passion-fruit

125 g/4 oz/½ cup caster (superfine) sugar

150 ml/¼ pint/⅔ cup water

1 mango

10 lychees, canned or fresh

1 star-fruit

1 Halve the passion-fruit and press the flesh through a sieve (strainer) into a saucepan.

2 Add the sugar and water to the pan and bring to a gentle boil, stirring.

3 Put the mango on a chopping board and cut a thick slice from either side, cutting as near to the stone (pit) as possible. Cut away as much flesh as possible in large chunks from the stone (pit) section.

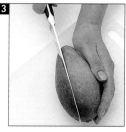

4 Take the 2 side slices and make 3 cuts through the flesh but not the skin, and 3 more at right angles to make a lattice pattern.

5 Push inside out so that the cubed flesh is exposed and you can easily cut it off.

6 Peel and stone (pit) the lychees and cut the star-fruit into 12 slices.

7 Add all the mango flesh, the lychees and star-fruit to the passion-fruit syrup and poach gently for 5 minutes. Remove the fruit with a perforated spoon.

8 Bring the syrup to the boil and cook for 5 minutes until it thickens slightly.

9 To serve, transfer all the fruit to individual serving glasses, pour over the sugar syrup and serve warm.

COOK'S TIP

A delicious accompaniment to any exotic fruit dish is cardamom cream. Crush the seeds from 8 cardamom pods, add 300 ml/½ pint/1¼ cups whipping cream and whip until soft peaks form.

Lime Mousse with Mango

Lime-flavoured cream moulds, served with a fresh mango and lime sauce, make a stunning dessert.

NUTRITIONAL INFORMATION

Calories . . . . . . .254 Sugars 17g
Protein . . . . .5g Fat 19g
Carbohydrate . . .17g Saturates 12g

10 MINS   0 MINS

SERVES 4

I N G R E D I E N T S

250 g/9 oz/1 cup fromage frais

grated rind of 1 lime

1 tbsp caster (superfine) sugar

125 ml/4 fl oz/½ cup double (heavy) cream

M A N G O   S A U C E

1 mango

juice of 1 lime

4 tsp caster (superfine) sugar

T O   D E C O R A T E

4 Cape gooseberries

strips of lime rind

1 Put the fromage frais, lime rind and sugar in a bowl and mix together.

2 Whisk the double (heavy) cream in a separate bowl and fold into the fromage frais.

3 Line 4 decorative moulds or ramekin dishes with muslin (cheesecloth) or cling film (plastic wrap) and divide the mixture evenly between them. Fold the muslin (cheesecloth) over the top and press down firmly.

4 To make the sauce, slice through the mango on each side of the large flat stone, then cut the flesh from the stone. Remove the skin.

5 Cut off 12 thin slices and set aside. Chop the remaining mango, put into a food processor with the lime juice and sugar. Blend until smooth. Alternatively, push the mango through a sieve (strainer) then mix with the lime juice and sugar.

6 Turn out the moulds on to serving plates. Arrange 3 slices of mango on each plate, pour some sauce around, decorate and serve.

COOK'S TIP

Cape gooseberries have a tart and mildly scented flavour and make an excellent decoration for many desserts. Peel back the papery husks to expose the bright orange fruits.

This is a Parragon Book
This edition published in 2003

Parragon
Queen Street House
4 Queen Street
Bath BA1 1HE, UK

Copyright © Parragon 2001

ISBN: 1-40540-107-9

Printed in China

NOTE

This book uses metric and imperial measurements. Follow the same units
of measurement throughout; do not mix metric and imperial.
All spoon measurements are level: teaspoons are assumed to be 5 ml, and
tablespoons are assumed to be 15 ml. Unless otherwise stated,
milk is assumed to be full fat, eggs and individual vegetables such as potatoes
are medium, and pepper is freshly ground black pepper.

The nutritional information provided for each recipe is per serving or per person.
Optional ingredients variations or serving suggestions have
not been included in the calculations. The times given for each recipe are an approximate
guide only because the preparation times may differ according to the techniques used by
different people and the cooking times may vary as a result of the type of oven used.

Recipes using raw or very lightly cooked eggs should be
avoided by infants, the elderly, pregnant women, convalescents,
and anyone suffering from an illness.

*The publisher would like to thank
Steamer Trading Cookshop, Lewes, East Sussex, for the kind loan of props.*